Music.
Not Noise

Pitch perfect leadership

G. Robert James

Copyright © 2024 G. Robert James
All rights reserved
First Edition

Fulton Books
Meadville, PA

Published by Fulton Books 2024

ISBN 979-8-89221-227-4 (paperback)
ISBN 979-8-89221-228-1 (digital)

Printed in the United States of America

Contents

Introduction v

Chapter 1: Get over Yourself—No One Is Immune to Adversity 1

Chapter 2: The New Kangaroo—Solve the Right Problem 13

Chapter 3: Thinking Counterintuitively—the Scourge of Unidimensional Thinking 21

Chapter 4: Turkeys in the Convocation— Inspiring Excellence 29

Chapter 5: The Carpenter Ant, the Fox, and the Dolphin—Work Hard and Smart 36

Chapter 6: The Cube Farm—the Fastest Way to Lose Constituents Is to Lose Touch with Them 40

Chapter 7: This Is What We Do—Selling Chicken and Cheerios 46

Chapter 8: Flat Squirrels—Lead. Follow. Or Get Out of the Way! 56

Chapter 9: Steak before Sizzle—Maslow Had a Point 61

Chapter 10: Make Me Money or Save Me Money— Focus on Fundamental Purpose 72

Chapter 11: Process Makes Perfect—Perfecting Fundamentals 76

Chapter 12: You Eat What You Kill—Hunt Wisely. Defend Diligently. Consume Efficiently. 83

Chapter 13: Control the Message, or It Will Control You—the Communication Imperative 93

Conclusion: The Mic Drop 105

Introduction

Anyone who has ever experienced a middle school orchestra recital often shares a pained smile when reminiscing. What we feel is usually a mixture of pride, uneasiness, and perhaps even emotional discomfort. What we hear is *noise*. In comparison, the experience at the symphony is commonly the opposite. What we feel is calm, admiration, and pleasure. What we hear is *music*.

Many reasons exist for the difference between music and noise. The children, although less experienced and possessing varying levels of talent, are playing their instruments with passion and determination. They practice hard and as often as possible. They are playing from the same sheet of music and are led by a passionate conductor. This is not significantly different from the more polished symphony. Granted, members of the symphony tend to be more experienced and talented than the middle schoolers. However, the mechanics are the same. Yet the symphony creates *music* while the middle schoolers are working their hearts out to produce something that usually sounds more like *noise*.

A key reason for the difference is that the symphony is playing passionately from each chair *together*, while the hopeful students are not. That is the biggest difference between music and noise. Businesses are another version of the orchestra. They consist of individuals focusing on their unique roles to produce a positive experience for their audiences—for customers, partners, and stakeholders. Whether conditions are favorable or challenging, the need to create music is constant. The discordance that noise creates can be obvious to many. However, only those with finely tuned hearing recognize soon enough what is out of tune and what to do about it. Those gifted with near-perfect pitch pay close attention not only to how

INTRODUCTION

their people synchronize but also to how systems, processes, and procedures synchronize as well. Effective leaders tend to have near-perfect pitch. Ineffective leaders tend to be tone-deaf.

Alexandre Dumas said that business is quite simple. "You make something and then sell it for more than it cost you to make…that and a few million details." The concept of commerce is timeless, even though the details are elusive and diverse, and they are constantly evolving. They are influenced by a litany of factors from the logical to the illogical—and everything in between. Importantly, many of the most critical details go unrecognized unless they make themselves obvious or leaders know what to listen for, where to look, and what to see and hear.

Throughout history, experts and academics have defined, dissected, tested, and debated a variety of philosophies and theories about commerce and leadership. Yet the core of Dumas's statement remains—no matter how hard we try to prove otherwise. Universally, organizations face challenges that require leadership skills beyond textbooks and tangibles. These skills foster a leadership mindset that accepts that certain assertions hold true.

- All organizations experience challenges at some point.
- Seeing and hearing what is not obvious is an uncommon but essential skill.
- Many of the most important indicators are subtle cues rarely found in lectures or books.
- Multidimensional vision is crucial. Selfish myopia is destructive.
- Focus on fundamentals is necessary.
- Adapt, evolve, or perish.

Inevitably, even the most accomplished organizations face adversity. Regardless of the growth stage, all organizations are affected by changing market dynamics and self-imposed challenges. To the executive, navigating the waters created by challenging factors can make course correction feel much like turning around a battleship in a bathtub. Depending on the situation, time constraints, financial resources, cultural nuances, and external pressures often make the fit tight and the waters toxic. Beyond business acumen and experience, successfully leading an organization through adversity requires vision, a multidimensional perspective, focus, inspiration, courage, determination, discipline, and luck. Lots and lots of luck.

Approaches to these challenges vary. Most important, however, is the importance of a *multidimensional perspective*. In the parable of the blind men and the elephant, a group of blind men heard that a strange animal called an elephant had been brought to the town, but none of them were aware of its shape and form. Out of curiosity, they agreed to inspect it for themselves. The first person encountered the elephant's trunk and determined it must be a snake. The second person reached out to find the elephant's ear and determined it must be some kind of fan. The next person reached out and found a leg and determined it must be a tree trunk. The next touched the elephant's side and announced it was a wall. The next person felt its tail and concluded the object was a rope. The final person felt a tusk and proclaimed the object to be a spear. These perspectives prevented them from recognizing the whole animal, thus rendering their assessments entirely inaccurate. Effective leaders see the whole organism, collecting and synthesizing all the internal and external components influencing the organization's performance. Importantly, these leaders recognize that adversity is typically caused by a variety of factors that are rarely mutually exclusive. As a result, these leaders consider the broader impacts and consequences of ideally multidimensional solutions. Tone-deaf leaders tend to invest energy and resources in a singular problem with a singular solution. Certainly, some challenges are clearly simple. Resisting the urge to overcomplicate requires clear thinking to prevent molehills from becoming insurmountable mountains. However, effective leaders begin with a macro-level view of the situation before zooming in on its components. Tone-deaf leaders tend to focus on the squeakiest instrument.

Most tone-deaf leaders fail to recognize the leading indicators that predict downturns, often because the organizational culture is overly myopic, unjustifiably confident, or simply refuses to accept reality. The oft-used "frog in the boiling pot" analogy illustrates the

INTRODUCTION

ease at which leaders can fall into the trap of comfort until an unanticipated existential challenge occurs. Many executives realize they are in a pot of water, get comfortable, and then realize the water has begun to boil before doing something to turn down the heat or get out of the water. As a result, the response can be slow and chaotic.

Tone-deaf leaders also typically misdiagnose performance indicators, which results in incomplete solutions and inefficient investment. During the course, executives apply solutions with which they are most familiar rather than challenge convention. However, prescriptive measures are only as effective as the holistic vision applied. Many examples of success and failure exist today. In all these, the results directly reflect the existence, or lack of, clear vision, discipline, sense of urgency, and courage.

Sustained success is part art and part craft. The most effective leaders tend to be those who are determined to make the complex simple rather than make the simple complex. They recognize the organism that is the organization. They share a practical vision to see future opportunities that have the highest potential to monetize big and small ideas quickly. They have the courage to dance to music few others hear, to see what is not there, and to think counterintuitively.

Not all organizations experience existential challenges. However, even the most successful organizations have experienced conditions requiring clear and decisive correction. In his theory of evolution, Darwin points out that it is the most adaptable that survives. Organizations are no different. To survive and thrive, organizations must be agile—in thought and action—so they can effectively and efficiently adapt when the time comes.

The significant wave of start-ups spawned by a global entrepreneurial boom has introduced a fresh collection of companies entering their first stage of business evolution. These entrepreneurs possess passion and courage that inspire them to pursue their dreams. They tend to be experts when it comes to their new concepts. They represent a new generation of better mousetrap builders. Start-up success rates clearly reflect the challenges these new entrepreneurs face. The most successful tend to be led by people who see and hear harmony in the systems, processes, and people in their organizations. Those who fail tend to struggle to create harmony. Certainly, many variables—both controllable and uncontrollable—ultimately contribute to the success or failure of a start-up. Undercapitalization. Market conditions. Competitive response. Many of those million details. However, the odds of success tend to increase when leadership creates multidimensional harmony.

Of course, sometimes dead is dead. The Buggy Whip Cemetery is crowded with some of the most memorable brands in history that failed to adapt. Of the Fortune 500 firms that existed in 1955, 88 percent have either gone bankrupt, merged to survive, or fallen from the Fortune 500 ranks. From A&P to Polaroid to Kodak to Pan Am Blockbuster to Toys R Us to the dozens of others trying to compete in an increasingly evolving environment, failure to adapt resulted in these once prominent battleships sinking or becoming an unrecognized version of their former selves. Despite the exhaustively analyzed explanations for these failures, a common core exists—a leadership mindset that failed to adapt and ignored the less obvious cues. They failed to hear the noise or thought the noise was music.

Conceptually, all organizations are similar. They consist of individuals of varying talents and experience working passionately to produce an outcome. High-performing organizations do so *together*. Distressed organizations, almost always, do not. Effective leaders can hear the difference. Every time. The key is to listen…*to sense*. Once this sense is refined, the noise becomes physically uncomfortable. This discomfort is the first indicator of the true reality. Beyond the financials. Beyond the stock performance. Beyond the efficiency reports. Beyond employee satisfaction. Beyond customer alerts. The noisy performance of an organization is the key indicator of distress. To the most astute leader, noisy performance just *feels* wrong.

In most ways, this noisiness is a symptom but quickly becomes the cause for inevitably greater adversity and existential threat. Astute leaders differentiate themselves by recognizing noisy performance as a *predictor* rather than an *indicator*. Their response is measured, decisive, resolved, and strategic. Tone-deaf leaders react to noise with superficial tactics, assumptions, and gut—if they react at all.

INTRODUCTION

Most prescriptive measures taught through schools, seminars, case studies, and shared are valuable resources for leaders seeking insight to fuel strategic decisions. What the professors, experts, and books teach, coupled with real life, are helpful. However, when addressing disharmony, a unique and honed instinct that recognizes intangible subtleties impacting performance that are not immediately obvious is imperative to recognizing and then transforming noise into music. It is an instinct that is often innate among the most effective leaders and contextualized through real-time experience. It is a perspective honed by experience, successes, and failures that separates exceptional leaders from tone-deaf leaders.

This is about that.

Chapter 1

Get over Yourself—No One Is Immune to Adversity

Effective leaders are inherently confident. They embody confidence. They exude confidence. They inspire confidence. Stakeholders—from employees to customers to partners—require the assurance that their livelihoods and futures are in competent hands. The fine line between self-confidence and cockiness is often blurred. This is natural. This is human. And it applies not only to the individuals within the organizations but to the entire organism which the individuals comprise.

The age of the indestructible brand is over. The brands that struggle to toe that fine line share common traits at the universal and individual levels. At the universal level, struggling icons find themselves in shock and disbelief when performance declines become impossible to ignore. Check the boneyard. We have forgotten more icons than we realize.

Distinguishing music from noise—particularly in complex organizations—is heavily influenced by an enterprise-wide openness to *really* listen and hear. One of the most common and blatant leadership weaknesses among struggling organizations is poor listening skills. Usually, these leaders tend to hear what they are listening for and see what they are looking for, which obscures the realities of the existing situation. These leaders tend to dominate conversations about solving problems, stifling valuable exchange of information and ideas that can result in creative solutions. As the Dalai Lama put it, "When you talk, you are only repeating what you know. When you listen, you may learn something new." The importance of listening with an open mind and without agenda is important in any instance but crucial when addressing adversity.

> *When addressing organizational performance concerns, does leadership seek input from multiple relevant corners and levels of the organization?*
> *Does leadership typically address adversity solitarily rather than collaboratively?*
> *How often do you hear "I can fix this" rather than "We can fix this"?*
> *In discussions regarding adverse conditions, do you hear "I" more than "we"?*
> *How willing are team members to speak the truth to power without fear of repercussion or ridicule?*
> *Is the immediate response of leadership denial?*
> *Do valuable team members hesitate to share solutions because they feel leadership will not listen or take action?*
> *Do you join meetings to address adverse conditions excited but leave them frustrated?*

Most ineffective leaders dismiss negative trends, touting their history and global power. They are convinced that they are too big to fail, and the rest of the organization buys in. No one wants to admit weakness or vulnerability. And stakeholders, while requiring transparent conversation of potential risks, do not want to hear about weaknesses.

Obviously, for many, invulnerability is no longer true. Just check the boneyard. Another common and often unnoticed characteristic among those who fail to recognize and evolve through adversity is that they talk to and about themselves rather than those they exist to serve. This behavior is usually gradual and fueled by success, as well as the absence of significant threats. Marketing, advertising, sales, operations, engineering, and R&D all talk about themselves rather than their role in the lives of their customers. They reward themselves for introspective performance, such as short-term productivity, rather than the more long-term goals. Marketing and advertising messages attempt to solidify consumer confidence by emphasizing the organization's size, history, and position rather than how the organization fits into their customers' lives. Quick and honest answers to a few simple questions often help leaders understand how much organizational arrogance exists.

> *Do we think our customers and partners need us to survive? Does our behavior reflect that belief?*
> *Are our failures frequently attributed to someone other than ourselves?*
> *Are external messages arrogant?*
> *Are rewards and incentives skewed toward introspective goals?*
> *What percentage of our trophy case consists of industry recognition of our greatness, compared to what we do for our customers?*
> *How much of our energy is spent on patting ourselves on the back?*
> *Do the causes of performance declines focus on external factors and less on internal attitudes?*
> *How often do we think that we are just too large to fail?*
> *Do we blame or belittle our customers when they complain? Is our response "They just don't understand what we do?"?*

Organizational narcissism does not resonate with most consumers. Importantly, it also creates operational struggles. Such is the case of a computer technology company that experienced rapid success after inventing a device that was widely appreciated by client companies worldwide. With limited competition and rapid growth, the operation began to focus on itself. Competition was limited, and all followed the company's lead as first to market. The sales force was exceptionally talented, and its confidence was bolstered by the first-to-market position. Engineering was creative and skilled. Sales grew. Market acceptance was exceptional, prompting a successful IPO that attracted a considerable number of market makers who increased the company's value at an unanticipated rate. This extraordinary success affected the culture. At the core, the company consisted of extraordinary people at every level. Humble. Dignified. Focused. Determined. Innovative. Just really good people. However, their messaging grew increasingly introspective, and a sense of invincibility became pervasive in a number of ways. One of the most destructive ways was product release mishaps. Competition and overconfidence drove the sales organization to promise releases that frequently missed their committed release dates. Missed release dates eroded customer and stakeholder confidence. Internally, arguments ensued. After several months of ignoring the real problem, the sales team ultimately pushed engineering for improved productivity. Engineering did not share the sense of urgency and insisted that the customer requirements were unreasonable. Both neglected the attitudinal contributor to a problem that quickly threatened their existence.

> *We're first. We can do no wrong.*
> *They need us more than we need them.*
> *They just don't understand what it takes to create this technology.*
> *These missed deadlines are not serious.*

As customers became increasingly frustrated by delays that affected their own performance, alternatives became increasingly viable. As the competition seized the opportunity to grab more share, sales and profitability suffered. As sales and profitability suffered, financial markets began to lose confidence. As the financial markets began to lose confidence, market makers took their positions elsewhere. The result was a penny stock designation, a significant decline in capitalization, and a loss of leadership position. Today, the company still exists. With its growth trajectory disrupted, it has returned to its original size, unlikely to ever regain its prominence. While many other variables contributed to this result, at the core was a pervasive sense of invincibility that never showed up on spreadsheets and financial statements.

In the case of Abercrombie & Fitch, once one of the trendiest casual wear and accessory brands of the new millennium, a seemingly valid strategy focusing on exclusivity became a pillar that employees and customers quickly found appealing. The retailer's primary target was influenced by the pop culture that shaped the way teens wanted to look, dress, and smell. An exclusive position worked well, but rapidly obvious consumer priorities magnified the weaknesses of the strategy. In 2006, Abercrombie & Fitch CEO Mike Jeffries stated, "Sex sells. That is why we hire good-looking people in our stores. Because good-looking people attract other good-looking people, and we want to market to cool, good-looking people. We don't market to anyone other than that." Another A&F leader was quoted as saying, "We would rather burn clothes than give them to poor people." This arrogance was pervasive within the A&F culture, and its consumers quickly branded A&F as "out of touch." Today, Abercrombie & Fitch continues to struggle to maintain a sustainable position.

Overconfidence always begins at the personal level. Ideally, leaders try to surround themselves with people who believe in themselves. Consequently, we believe in them. We trust them. This confidence and trust results in constant reassurance that assigned responsibilities at all levels of an organization are effectively managed. Of course, common business practice requires safety nets in the form of performance evaluation processes and human capital development and growth programs designed to establish measurable goals that contribute to the overall objective and provide clear procedures to address opportunity areas. Ideally.

In distressed organizations, pervasive overconfidence and the emotionally driven focus on self-preservation commonly complicate efforts to correct course at all levels. Individuals cling relentlessly to their belief that they are doing a good job. Like the poor carpenter who blames the failure on tools, materials, or other issues, members of the organizations cling to the belief that they are doing everything right as one clings to air to breathe. Again, it is natural. People work to live rather than live to work. Effective leaders recognize a subtle yet destructive attitudinal undertone—focus on the person rather than the organization. This self-centric shift becomes increasingly evident as conditions worsen and are recognizable at all levels of the organization. The key is to get over yourself.

If you are so competent, why is your business struggling?

Certainly, external factors affect the distress. Effective leaders anticipate most of these factors and plan for them. As conditions worsen, the instinctive response is to invest an inordinate amount of time and money in the cause rather than the solution. It is a bit like quicksand. The harder they struggle to swim out, the deeper they sink. Rather than soberly addressing escape options, tone-deaf leaders flail to fail.

The Great Atlantic & Pacific Tea Company (A&P) is one of the iconic retail brands that now occupies a spot in the boneyard and exhibits this destructive attitude to the point of extinction. They enjoyed a brilliant history of growth as a meaningful part of the communities they served. Through organic growth and acquisition, they arguably became the foundation of food retailing in North America for generations. And then the landscape changed. Competition fought harder and smarter to entrench themselves in battleground neighborhoods. Mass merchants commoditized the food retailing industry in a way that leadership had never seen before and refused to acknowledge as a meaningful shift in consumer requirements. Channel blurring blinded leadership across all ranks. The landscape changed rapidly, and leadership failed to adapt and evolve with that change quickly enough.

Early external indicators clearly alerted them to trouble. Despite adamant insistence from the incumbent Chairman and CEO to pay attention to and present solutions for what he recognized as real existential threats, most of the leaders refused to accept the valid insight. Most of them spent extensive energy disputing and discrediting the information. When presented with mounting data and insights supporting the uncomfortable realities, most of them resorted to the tried-and-true tactic of demanding more data, generally a stall tactic that creates data fatigue and decision-making paralysis. Merchandising leaders refused to accept that they had a poor price image that was prompting customers to consider alternatives for their food. Operations leaders refused to believe that customers were disillusioned with poor service and uninspiring facilities.

We invented this industry. We know what the market wants better than it knows itself.

We are known for always giving our customers the best quality, even though it costs a little more.

My stores are clean, and my people reflect my commitment to quality service every day.

We've been around for generations. Our customers will always be loyal to us.

But they were not. During the economic crisis of the mid-2000s, leaders of the company quickly blamed alarming declines on the economy at board meetings and on quarterly conference calls with Wall Street. As the trends continued, they blamed everything and everyone but themselves, promising bold and aggressive plans to secure the confidence of stakeholders. They were saving their own hides, not because they were bad people, but because the idea that they were personally responsible for failures was inconceivable. They were. Although others may have been responsible for executional lapses, leadership was accountable. Declining execution standards were a symptom rather than a cause. Most significantly, responsibility for ignoring the warning signs that were revealed long before the downturn fell directly into their laps. To quote Warren Buffett, "Only when the tide goes out do you learn who has been swimming naked." Apparently, a large number of leaders fancied skinny dipping. They soon lost their jobs. Top-tier talent was easily poached by competitors. Those who remained secured lucrative retention incentives in a further attempt to stem a massive and devastating exodus. Top-tier prospects only agreed to join the obviously struggling ship under extremely expensive conditions. Negative customer trends accelerated. Investors grew increasingly impatient. Leadership responded with ineffective, generally superficial conventional tactics. They panicked as their options rapidly diminished. Ultimately, the company did something that shocked the industry and will be a teachable case study for years to come—it perished.

Most effective leaders address adversity very simply—they first look in the mirror. Walking the fine line between confidence and cockiness is especially delicate at this stage. Overly expressed or, worse, insincere humility quickly erodes the confidence internal and external stakeholders demand of leadership. Importantly, pride is one of the most common—albeit human—impediments to successful performance. It is not easy to accept failure. It is even more difficult to admit our failure to others. Genuine, introspective evaluation is essential.

At the top, leaders are held accountable. Whether to boards, investors, families, or a mix of many, the pressures borne by top leaders are immense. Heavy is the head that wears the crown. Above all, leaders are accountable to themselves. The most effective leaders recognize the signs of distress before the pressures become intense. Most leaders, however, find themselves feeling the weight of these pressures after the pot has already begun to boil. The causes for this are numerous. Most often, the information they receive is tainted with denial. Organizations often lack leaders courageous enough to speak the truth to power, or power refuses to accept the unflattering truth. Regardless, leadership at the top becomes caught in a vice between external and internal pressures. Self-preservation and self-confidence inspire these leaders to passionately argue their ability to correct the trajectory. Getting past the focus on "self" is common among those who are successful.

Unfortunately, self-preservation, while natural, is destructive. Most leaders who focus on saving their jobs and reputations eventually fail. Many immediately direct attention to external factors over which they have no control. Whether the conditions relate to the economy, new competition, regulatory issues, internal failures, or thousands of other reasons, self-preservation prompts these leaders to focus on reasons. Very often, these leaders can prolong the inevitable personal failure—termination—by making notable organizational changes in the form of changes in the organizational structure, termination of key management and other personnel, and other diversionary tactics. Ultimately, these diversionary tactics prevent the organization from more promptly addressing the challenge and almost always result in the inevitable—failure.

Self-confidence is also a common, slightly less destructive, behavior among these leaders. They have recognized the realities and have acknowledged the need to address the solutions soberly, promptly, and decisively. However, a false sense of confidence often convinces these leaders to believe that they, alone, are the ones to correct the trajectory. Objective stakeholders typically view this attitude skeptically, pointing out the reality that the current conditions exist on their watch. The buck, indeed, stops at the top. When the CEO tells the board that he or she is the only person to correct a negative trajectory—either blatant or inferred—failure is imminent. It is rare to find one person who can master every instrument in the orchestra.

The key is to listen and watch. A tone-deaf leader is a poor conductor. Getting caught in the trap of diversion and distraction is easy but destructive. Leadership focuses on causes, and self are critical indicators and require quick and decisive attention. Leaders who blame the economy or constantly direct conversations to their own talent and accomplishments will fail. Leaders who distract and deflect will fail. Those who are enlightened enough to get over themselves stand a greater chance of successfully saving the distressed organization. Those who are successful recognize the instinctive tendency to think about themselves but redirect their focus on the solutions necessary to sensibly correct the negative trends. These leaders keep the organization ahead of themselves. Most importantly, this behavior is part of their leadership style, inspiring stakeholders at all levels to dismiss selfish urges in the interest of the organization. They inspire all stakeholders to recognize that this selflessness is in their self-interest. If the selflessness of the stakeholders is successful, their livelihoods are preserved.

Selfless leadership is often effective. Generally, no one deliberately causes an organization to become distressed. While people can sometimes make meaningful mistakes, most organizations consist of people who want to do a good job and contribute to the success of the organization. Sometimes, the best intentions are not enough. Whether at the departmental, divisional, or corporate levels, distress occurs. Harnessing dedicated talent with mission clarity, selfless determination, and decisive actions enhances the potential for success.

Of course, people are people. Many are just selfish. Perhaps as many are selfless. In either case, the human condition requires that we provide for ourselves and our families, and we feel good about ourselves. This guarantees that people think about themselves first. Some will get over themselves for the sake of the whole. Most will not. Among those who do not, many will lose their passion for the cause and often abandon ship. Those who lose their passion are essentially waiting for the outcome without investing themselves in contributing. They leave work unfinished. They are less diligent about excellence. They make mistakes uncommon in their history. They realize the realities but do not seem to care. Many of these people leave at the first opportunity. Until then, they are being paid but not performing. The number of unemployed people on the payroll of struggling companies is alarming.

Recognizing those who refuse to get over themselves is critical. Recognizing the overly self-confident or self-centered requires open eyes and decisive action. The most common indicator is unproductive focus on "who's right" rather than "what's right." When addressing issues of concern, many meetings become bogged down in conversations about whose idea is the right one to resolve the problems. Effective leaders quickly recognize the noisiness of these conversations and redirect focus to what is right. Tone-deaf leaders fail to hear the noise and ultimately allow the loudest voice or most tenured individuals to dominate decisions.

> *How many times did this conversation focus on the person rather than the purpose?*
> *Is the advocacy really addressing what the right solution should be, or are my leaders herding in support of a personal or group affiliation?*

John F. Kennedy once said, "We must think like men and women of action and act like men and women of thought." When the audiences stop swaying to your music and you struggle to attract virtuosos, act thoughtfully. At the top, addressing personal selflessness should be the first course of action. Stakeholders responsible for governance should address the chief executive with similar scrutiny. These governors should anticipate the common *tendency of self* in the chief executive and provide thoughtful guidance to avoid costly tactical errors through the loss of valuable talent and ineffective strategies. Likewise, leadership at all levels within the organization should act similarly, forsaking selfishness and focusing on thoughtful action. The most effective leaders have been those who

- ask the uncomfortable questions of themselves to genuinely address personal shortcomings and choices contributing to the adversity,
- listen closely for "me" speak and "I" declarations, and
- eliminate fear.

Self-reflection is the most difficult place to begin, but it is the only place to begin. Anything else is putting the cart before the horse. Most effective leaders find it easy to ask themselves how their decision or leadership style contributed to the current situation. These leaders exude confidence and competence in an authentically humble way. For some, such authentic humility is just natural. Others choose to surround themselves with people, such as coaches, mentors, and advisers, who have the courage and character to push them to continuously grow through introspection. Sycophants need not apply. For all, sincere reflection inspires them to demonstrate their humanity openly and honestly without eroding organizational confidence in the leader. It sparks a culture that loses its ego.

Adverse conditions trigger a natural pattern of self-validation. Everyone prefers to think that the problem is somewhere else, either internally or externally. In any organization struggling through adversity, "me" speak and "I" declarations are prevalent. Tone-deaf leaders miss the significance of their existence. Effective leaders do not. Effective leaders quickly notice how increasingly often "me" and "I" are part of every discussion. They act to quickly eliminate the attitude of the people. Often this attitude is destructive and severely inhibits any chance of fighting through the adverse conditions. Depending on the degree of challenge, choosing whether to adjust the attitude or eliminate the individual must happen quickly and decisively. Change the attitude or eliminate the person.

While ego is often a culprit in a selfish organizational culture, the more common driver is the survival instinct. Every time a leader confronts the organization to address declining performance, self-validation becomes rampant for a variety of reasons. Effective leaders recognize this human condition and address it early in a variety of ways. Fabrizio Freda, CEO of the Estée Lauder Companies, possesses all these essential qualities and addresses the fear of failure very simply. "Fail fast, fail cheap" is his consistent directive. This cultural attitude inspires his organization to have the courage to make bold but measured choices. It tells the teams that failure, while not ideal, is acceptable—as long as the sponsor does not throw good money after bad. It is a selfless mindset that removes the distraction of selfishness. Identify the challenge. Act fearlessly. Measure. Deal with the personnel issues separately.

Fear is even more prevalent in terms of communication—particularly during difficult times. The exposure of fault and flaw is quickly personalized, fostering an instinctive communication culture that consists of "spin" and omission. The most effective leaders are those who have instilled a culture that believes that there is no such thing as bad news. When leaders in successful organizations realize that the message is unlikely going to cost them their jobs, but failure to communicate the truth will, fear-driven information and communication are less likely to contribute to failure.

Every organization consists of people. People are inherently self-driven. Even the most enlightened of us has self-service as a key motivator. Adversity triggers the survival mechanism in all of us. Leadership that recognizes the human condition but identifies and eliminates destructive, self-serving behaviors is critical to leading an organization through adversity. It is difficult and must begin at the top to establish a selfless culture. Personal relationships, pack mentality, and alpha personalities compound the challenge and potentially generate silent noise. Most importantly, the ability to compartmentalize business from emotion is essential. Effective leaders insist on addressing *what's* right. Tone-deaf leaders waste time addressing *who's* right.

Chapter 2

The New Kangaroo—Solve the Right Problem

There is the story of the zoo that recently acquired a rare and prized kangaroo. The board was extremely proud of this rare acquisition and authorized capital and other essential resources to build the most impressive, state-of-the-art enclosure ever created. Every zoo would be envious, and every guest would be impressed.

The president handled every detail of the exhibit personally, insisting on perfection in every aspect. After months of tedious design and construction, the enclosure was ready for its occupant. A week before opening, the kangaroo was introduced to his new home so that he could acclimate and familiarize himself.

The morning after, the zookeeper opened the park to find his prize acquisition bounding freely about the grounds.

"Oh, no!" the zookeeper exclaimed. "Our kangaroo has escaped his enclosure. We have less than a week to fix this. Build the wall higher!"

So the design and construction teams immediately began adding height to the enclosure wall. After two days of construction, the wall was finished. The zookeeper reintroduced his kangaroo to the exhibit. To his dismay, the zookeeper returned the next day to find his feisty kangaroo bouncing across the grounds.

"It's still not tall enough," the zookeeper told his team. "Build it higher."

His teams responded quickly, working around the clock to add more height to the wall. Amid all the frantic activity, the friendly giraffe in the enclosure next door leaned over the growing wall to visit his neighbor.

"How tall do you think they're going to build this wall?" he asked the kangaroo.

"I have no idea," the kangaroo replied. "Probably as tall as it takes them to realize that I'm not jumping the wall. They keep leaving my gate open."

Leaders who are responsible for correcting declining performance must identify and address the problems quickly. In the best of cases, they collect information, diagnose causes, and develop actionable plans to correct the issues. Teams are formed. Reports are produced. In the best scenarios, success metrics are developed. More often than one might imagine, many organizations misdiagnose the cause. This results in ineffective solutions. The resulting plans are not always bad. They just address the wrong problem. They built the wall higher because they failed to realize the gate was open.

The reasons for misdiagnosis vary. Self-preservation, misinformation, focus on symptoms rather than causes, reluctance to speak the truth to power, and short-sighted perspectives are among a plethora of factors that can contribute to misdiagnosis. Many organizations that fail to correct declining performance share these characteristics. The ultimate cost of misdiagnosis includes the loss of valuable time and limited resources. The cost of a bad plan is exponential.

Einstein once said, "If I had one hour to save the world, I would spend fifty-five minutes defining the problem and only five minutes finding the solution." Defining the problem is often uncomplicated. However, particularly among organizations in distress, defining the *real* problem is elusive. As Steve Jobs pointed out, "If you define the problem correctly, you almost have the solution."

The simple first question to ask about a correction plan is "Are we addressing the real problem? Has anyone checked to make sure the kangaroo isn't simply walking through an unlocked gate?" While hard to believe, this question is not always asked. Whether it is because everyone assumes someone else asked the questions, urgency causes hasty conclusions, the symptoms monopolize the analysis, or a variety of other reasons, the question does not always get asked. Whatever the case, effective solutions address the right problem. Effective leaders ask the right questions and challenge their teams to do the same.

> *Did anyone check the gate?*
> *Have we eliminated the simple answers?*
> *Are we overcomplicating the causes?*
> *Are we oversimplifying the causes?*

Survivorship bias is one of the most common culprits that misdirects leaders as they attempt to correct troubling trends. Too often, organizations dismiss blatant indicators that suggest uncomfortable solutions because they were not problems in the past. However, times change.

Simply put, survivorship bias occurs when we concentrate on success indicators and develop strategies based on these without holistically reviewing negative indicators as well. The well-documented case study regarding the influence of survivorship bias in designing military aircraft clearly illustrates the value of making sure the right issue is being addressed. During World War II, the military asked mathematician Abraham Wald to study how to best protect airplanes from being shot down. The military knew armor would help but could not protect the entire plane because over-armoring the craft would make it too heavy to fly well. Initially, military leaders planned to analyze planes returning from combat to see where they were hit worst. Their attention was immediately drawn to the wings, the area around the tail gunner, and down the center of the fuselage. The plan would be to reinforce those areas.

Wald pointed out that survivorship bias was misleading their thinking because the analysis neglected more valuable data—the planes that had not returned. He concluded that this misdirection motivated military leaders to fortify the wrong areas of the plane. The bullet holes they were looking at actually revealed the areas where a plane could be hit and continue flying. These areas did not require reinforcement. Instead, Wald inspired designers to fortify the areas of the surviving planes that were least hit. He pointed out that these areas were more likely the weak points that cost lives and equipment. This approach—solving the right problem—resulted in stronger aircraft and minimized loss.

There are many examples of survivorship bias in everyday life. Many parents today struggle with the debates with children who use Beyoncé, Kanye, Bill Gates, and Mark Zuckerburg as examples of people who did not need to finish college to be successful. Exclusive focus on successful stock trades often leads inexperienced traders to take irresponsible risks. The exclusive focus on success indicators, rather than comprehensively evaluating, rarely yields positive results.

Commercially, survivorship bias is possibly more prevalent now than ever before. Technology and data-savvy leadership have driven organizations to increasingly appreciate the value of and considerable dependence on information and insights. However, typical with such advancements, the resources often misdirect many leaders, steering them directly into the path of survivorship bias. One sector in which this is prevalent is retail. Regardless of industry, retailers ultimately recognized the importance of enhanced insights provided by a growing arsenal of data resources. The introduction of customer databases via loyalty cards pervades this sector as retailers clamor to find value in the new technology. Most often with the help of budding "experts," embraced the resource, creating custom segmentation schemes and strategies designed to solidify customer relationships. They created tiers. They customized incentives. They monetized each segment.

In the early days, most retailers struggled to understand how to effectively use the resources. They focused their attention on their most valuable customers, whether determined by volume, profitability, or other indicators. The survivors. Strategies focused on these customers with the intention of protecting the retailer's cash cows. However, many retailers who employed this approach quickly experienced profitability declines. They were giving away money through incentives to customers who did not need them. Meanwhile, the customers who were viable but vulnerable gradually spent elsewhere. Because these retailers concentrated exclusively on their best customers—survivors—they failed to recognize the viable but vulnerable customers. When they finally did, it was too late.

Conversely, retailers such as Kroger, Safeway, and Target viewed the insights these new databases provided holistically and developed CRM strategies that rewarded their most loyal customers but invested wisely in their viable but potentially vulnerable segments with meaningful offers and loyalty-building initiatives. Their focus on the areas of the plane that were least hit, thus identifying the real issue and removing survivorship bias, enabled them to apply the most effective approach.

Personal or philosophical bias is another reason leaders misidentify the true problem, thus prompting ineffective solutions. Whether because of deflection or a variety of other motivations, personal opinions, and agendas are common cancers that lead to failure. Particularly amid adversity, chaotic conditions often stir emotional reactions that are commonly fueled by personal bias. As a result, leaders fail to see the true issue. And they keep building taller walls.

One of many ongoing debates in the United States revolves around "Made in America." A popular discussion that ignites and polarizes American society, the topic has significant economic and patriotic implications. Politicians from every point in the ideological spectrum seize upon the subject to incite their bases. The problem has existed for decades. At the core is a very simple challenge—American society has experienced a difficult trend of job loss as companies outsource to other countries. Particularly in the manufacturing sector, American society has experienced a destructive exodus of companies to foreign nations, rendering the landscape a collective ghost town where thriving factories once existed.

The debate tends to concentrate on the countries to which these jobs are going and the decline in consumer demand for insistence on buying products made in America. Many are quick to demonize the countries to which these jobs have gone. Yet the debates continue as solutions blindly address the "culprit" nations. However, little analysis is devoted to the root causes of job exodus, as leaders focus on building taller walls rather than first checking the gate. Why are these jobs really leaving?

Few leaders acknowledge the reality that these business decisions are made by companies seeking solutions to enhance profitability rather than opportunistic countries working to improve their own economies. After all, it is far easier and more popular to demonize foreign entities than to acknowledge our own role in allowing the kangaroo to escape.

A quick check on the security of the gate, rather than the walls, reveals that simple economic decisions will take priority over nationalism in almost every instance. Simply put, companies are required to sell products and services for more than it costs to produce them. Shareholders and stakeholders demand this. Leaders are compensated based largely on profitability. The cost of providing goods and services increases organically. Additionally, price elasticity creates limitations, as consumers dictate how much a company can charge in an increasingly commoditized economy. Every aspect of COGS experiences inflation, forcing leaders to seek reductions through overhead and various other cost mitigation initiatives. Workers seek higher wages and benefits to provide for their families. Consumers seek more value as they continuously stretch limited dollars. Suppliers, landlords, and bankers systematically increase the cost of doing business, further chipping into profit margins. The increasing cost of doing business, along with shrinking revenue elasticity, squeezes business leaders, forcing them to make difficult and unpopular choices. Countries are not taking jobs; business leaders are giving them away. These culprit countries are simply a viable alternative to economic pressures. Economic pressures force leaders to give these jobs away. However, the most convenient focus for politicians is to focus on the countries rather than the true underlying cause of job exodus.

The emotional appeal of nationalism obscures focus and distracts leaders from identifying effective solutions. Because of this distraction, the debates remain perennial, circular, and unproductive. As the energy continues to focus on the walls around the country, the kangaroo continues to hop through the gate.

As damaging as overcomplication can be, the true issues creating discord can be complex. Oversimplifying the situation can lead to superficial solutions that ultimately fail to solve the problem.

In the case of United Technologies, confusion threatened capitalization. Through years of aggressive diversification, the company acquired a number of aircraft- and aircraft-component-manufacturing companies, including Sikorsky Aviation, Stearman Aircraft, Avion (later Northrop Aircraft), Chance Vought (aircraft), Hamilton (propellers and aircraft), and Pratt & Whitney (engines). Over the years, the company expanded and contracted its diverse portfolio to include brands such as Otis and Carrier. The brand portfolio became massive and complex. Despite continuous growth, capital markets failed to recognize the optimal value of the company. Many companies facing similar difficulties immediately develop complex strategies aimed at convincing Wall Street that they are worth more than analysts give them credit for. In this instance, that was not the approach.

Leadership concluded that the reason Wall Street valuation was below expectations was that those watching the company were confused. They recognized that the true issue was a lack of appreciation for the value of the *portfolio* despite brand performance. The portfolio of impressive brands was so strong that the investment community cringed at the noisiness. Conventional arguments advocated a lengthy and costly program to educate Wall Street about the value of each brand within the portfolio. Their stories were impressive. But the issue was with the portfolio, not its entities. Explaining the value of each individual instrument is meaningless to someone who just wants to hear music.

Rather than risk extensive resources in an attempt to teach and convince Wall Street to recognize the collective value of the forest, the company's leaders created a more comprehensive identity. Thus, it became United Technologies. The identity system subordinated each business unit to the parent brand, creating a unified identity that effectively simplified the complexity created by such a diverse portfolio. The result was market capitalization improvements. Investors better understand what the company does through its diverse brands. Rather than building the wall higher, these leaders checked the gate. They solved the right problem.

In the case of Motorola, failure to check the gate first resulted in a dramatic competitive slide from which the company has yet to fully recover. Once a leader in mobile communications, the company recognized competitive pressures that were suggesting a growing demand for smartphone technology. However, Motorola focused its innovation resources on aesthetics, choosing form over function. By the time the company finally released its own version of the smartphone, iPhone, Blackberry, and Samsung had disrupted the market with their own smartphones, replacing Motorola at the top of the Mobile Mountain. Consequently, the company's shares fell by 90 percent between October 2006 and March 2009, costing the company over $4 billion in value. While the new Motorola continues to operate, Samsung and iPhone have likely permanently replaced the once-recognized mobile phone leader.

Once the true causes are identified, the solutions will be more effective. Then it is a matter of execution, measurement, and refinement. That, and a few million other details. Pinpointing the real problem is rarely easy, especially in organizations in the throes of battle that forces them to spend more energy on mopping the floor rather than turning off the faucet. A multitude of factors and diverse perspectives complicate the process and can exacerbate troubling performance. Additionally, the existence of only one problem is rare, often creating confusion and distraction. The result is a multifront war against malicious gremlins who thrive on chaos. To successfully fight the battles, courage, resolve, and decisiveness are critical. Most effective leaders possess these qualities.

In addition to these, a critical quality effective leaders possess is the ability to make the complex simple, even though it is common for organizations to make the simple complex. Occam's Razor is the key. The most effective leaders begin there.

Are we addressing the real problem?

Once they inspire the organization to check the lock on the gate first, the next steps become far easier. Identifying the real issue with diverse thinking that eliminates bias, rather than solutions that fit familiar skill sets, improves the chances that the true problem will be solved.

Chapter 3

Thinking Counterintuitively—the Scourge of Unidimensional Thinking

People who are only good with hammers see every challenge as a nail. Organizations are necessarily comprised of many such people offering specialized skills and thinking. Properly applied, leaders can leverage individual talents and thought to create harmony with people, processes, and systems. Whether the skills are specific to a function or an individual, effective leaders recognize and leverage the unique functional and intellectual value at their disposal.

Adversity often prompts people to revert to thought and action that is most familiar to them. This guides leaders to address adversity with conventional solutions. They tend to think in one dimension. By definition, conventional solutions tend to lack creativity in favor of comfort and familiarity. But familiarity is fickle. They are usually solutions that often contribute to the current adverse conditions or were applied in the past with limited success. Many reasons exist for this tendency toward unidimensionality. Whatever the reason, adversity intensifies monomania.

Established organizations endure periods of evolution through which they learn to improve and grow. Successful organizations evolve quickly and inspire multidimensional thinking, which often results in exceptionally creative solutions to a variety of challenges. This evolution allows them to apply their talents and knowledge to drive continuing success. However, unidimensional thinking often

THINKING COUNTERINTUITIVELY

disrupts even the best business models. After all, "if it ain't broke, don't fix it."

Adversity forces leaders to evaluate their practices. However, most leaders only apply what they know. These solutions are frequently ineffective. To paraphrase Einstein, "If you keep doing what you've always done, you'll keep getting what you've always gotten." They do what they have always done but expect different results. They are the hammers. Their challenges are nails. The most effective leaders are those who look beyond convention and inspire their stakeholders to prudently consider all options—no matter how counterintuitive.

Diverse thinking is often absent in the wake of adversity. Myopic perspective, comfort, and intensified risk aversion create a paralytic impediment to organizational sustainability. Rampant among dysfunctional organizations is an attitude of *ttwadiism*. "That's the way we've always done it" is a common answer to why processes, procedures, strategies, and daily decisions occur as they do. A culture of ttwwadiism is almost always a common element in struggling organizations. Certainly, many of these practices may have been effective through the years, suggesting them as intuitively reasonable choices. However, something is no longer working. Changing *what* you do is rarely the issue. Changing *how you do what you do* is the issue. Donald Sull calls this "active inertia."

"Active inertia is an organization's tendency to follow established patterns of behavior—even in response to dramatic environmental shifts. Stuck in the modes of thinking and working that brought success in the past, market leaders simply accelerate their tried-and-true activities. In trying to dig themselves out of a hole, they just deepen it."

The difficulty is that many leaders do not know what they do not know, and too few press their organizations to explore solutions beyond the conventional—to think counterintuitively. The seasoned industry executive or the brilliant software developer is limited by his or her own knowledge, experience, and capabilities. Thus, all solutions are limited to what they know—pounding nails.

Knowledge, instinct, and experience almost always steer leaders toward conventional solutions and away from anything that simply does not seem to make sense. For example, the immediate response of retailers who face profit margin erosion is usually to raise retail prices, cut labor, and reduce promotional costs. Immediately, transactions decline due to diminished value perception, poor quality of service, and lackluster value offerings, accelerating the overall declines. Additionally, profit margins decline as transactions become exclusively limited to low-margin bargains. Thus begins the spiral. Like a person struggling to get out of quicksand, most retailers respond to these results by further continuing to "margin up" and deeper cost reduction.

One example is Toys R Us. While the cause of the icon's demise was complex and included many of the variables almost every seasoned executive has experienced, a component of their strategy that accelerated the spiral involved obvious conventional solutions. Fueled by the invasion of Walmart and other discount retailers into the toy segment, the industry became highly commoditized. This commoditization made the price the nail in the eyes of the executives. Although some immediate price corrections ensued, the inability to sustain margin demands prompted executives to seek relief through cost cutting. The obvious opportunities included store closures, inventory reduction, and labor cuts. The retailer reduced its market presence through an ineffective store closure strategy, removing itself from the minds of the target consumer. The stores that remained were tasked with supporting the entire brand but had fewer choices for the consumer, and labor cuts resulted in a diminished customer experience. In the end, the place where childhood whimsy and entertainment abounded became a warehouse filled with stuff that people preferred to buy from cheaper sources. No magic. No whimsy. Just expensive stuff. The continuing spiral fed more reactionary solutions that simply made the brand increasingly irrelevant to its loyal customers. In trying to dig themselves out of a hole, they just deepened it.

Had executives been afforded the time and the resources to think counterintuitively, the results could have been different. Of course, the debt load ultimately broke their backs. However, the debt might not have been a factor had executives explored unconventional solutions more quickly.

Perhaps if executives at Toys R Us had implemented SKU rationalization, retail labor rationalization, and outlet rationalization strategies early, they could have taken better control of the mounting debt pressures and given them more time to develop and implement other strategies necessary to ensure sustained competitiveness.

This approach does not mean the response to declining performance is to lower prices, increase promotions, and add labor. It means leaders should develop data-driven inventory and pricing and promotion strategies and seek labor solutions that deploy appropriate hours in a manner that prioritizes the customer experience and enhances operational efficiency. It means altering real estate strategies to evolve with shifting industry, consumer, and market dynamics to enhance investment efficiency. Conventional thinking identified each solution as a nail. The echo of the pounding hammer resounds in the halls of the empty space that was once a vibrant company.

Conventional thinking in the retail industry fears unconventional solutions. Margining up quickly delivers sales and margin increases. Labor reductions cut immediate costs. They do what they know. They hammer everything, whether it is a nail or a screw. The short-term benefits are generally short-lived and often compound the overall problem.

Counterintuitive thinking is about seeing what is not there and finding alternatives that are not always in the existing toolbox. Again, this does not mean organizations should change what they do. It does not mean that organizations should change simply for the sake of change. Counterintuitive thinking inspires a mindset that accepts possibilities beyond tradition and norms. Counterintuitive thinking expands the toolbox. It adds dimension. Effective leaders recognize that if they change the way they look at things, the things they look at change. Adversity tends to blind that view and stifle potentially effective counterintuitive thinking and behavior.

In the case of Burnham Service Corporation, counterintuitive thinking sparked a period of extraordinary growth. In 1921, L. R. Burnham founded his namesake Burnham Service Corporation in Columbus, Georgia. In the 1940s, the company expanded its core competency through Burnham Warehouses Inc. and Burnham

World Forwarders, the latter serving as the international arm. This growth continued into the 1960s. Relatively small by global standards, the company still enjoyed continued growth, reaching $10 million in revenue from over fifty branches by the late 1970s. Their core competency entrenched them as household movers, capitalizing on housing booms and family migration trends sparked by the opportunity presented in growing coastal cities. However, competition forced leadership to consider options to sustain growth.

Conventional thinking steered the company's leaders toward conventional solutions. Their specialization and success in moving and warehousing households inspired comfortable approaches. Open more branches. Open more warehouses. However, some members of the leadership team added dimension to their thinking. Making sure that they prevented any potentially harmful departures from their core competencies, management expanded its customer base by expanding its positioning. First, they established themselves as a *transportation and distribution services provider*, as opposed to a *moving company*. Management effectively reinforced the more dimensional positioning internally. Drivers, warehouse personnel, and support staff passionately evolved from a "moving company" to a company that provided comprehensive transportation and distribution services to individuals and organizations alike. What they did day in and day out may not have changed significantly. But how they thought and how they did what they did changed considerably. Next, they aggressively sought and established partnerships with the burgeoning computer hardware industry, securing a substantial agreement to warehouse and distribute IBM computers. They invested heavily in infrastructure that supported the partnership, integrating technology and people to efficiently fulfill customer needs with the precision of the German rail system. This counterintuitive transformation resulted in substantial growth. By 1987, revenues exceeded $100 million through eighty branches and more than one thousand employees. While industry consolidation has since changed the company entirely, counterintuitive thinking allowed them to withstand a potentially devastating competitive onslaught and expand their future possibilities.

Then there is Kodak. The company once dominated the photographic film market during most of the twentieth century. Leadership was the hammer; film was the nail. Ironically, Kodak engineers are often credited with inventing the first digital camera in 1975. However, leadership dismissed the new technology essentially because they failed to understand it. Filmless technology was not a nail. Additionally, this lack of understanding generated paralytic trepidation among leadership and management ranks. Kodak could have introduced filmless technology, but leadership was afraid that any potential traction would cannibalize the film market. Management was so focused on the film's success that they missed the digital revolution after starting it. Kodak filed for bankruptcy in 2012.

Counterintuitive thinking is risky. Along with myopia, fear is the primary barrier. Effective leaders seek unconventional thought. Effective leaders challenge themselves and their teams to open their minds and challenge conventional wisdom. Effective leaders see, hear, and act on multiple dimensions. Tone-deaf leaders are unidimensional.

The important thing to recognize is that counterintuitive solutions are not the entire answer; counterintuitive *thinking* is. Many of the unconventional solutions should not be applied because they simply do not work or apply. Many of these solutions have been tested and discarded. The most effective leaders are those who challenge conventional thinking and apply a carefully considered mix of conventional and unconventional solutions.

Another example of destructive conventional thinking is the food retail industry. As the landscape has shifted rapidly, solutions have not. As supermarket chains have realized rapid intrusion by untraditional competitors, the response tactics of most have remained traditional. With increased competition came the transition to commoditization. Quickly, consumers could find the same core products much more easily and cheaply at a new number of sources. The traditional response of most merchandising leaders has been to keep pounding the nail. The focus became margin driven. Prices were raised. Labor hours were cut. Manufacturers were pressed to contribute more merchandising income to compensate for margin declines.

Price increases, which only widened the price perception chasm among consumers, resulted in quick sales gains but cost transactions and market share. Conventional labor cuts resulted in customer service declines and decreased customer appreciation for the personal touch.

Increased focus on merchandising income yielded quick relief but became short-lived as manufacturers evolved their own financial models, consequently reducing the free flow of cash to retailers. Ultimately, bloated infrastructures and adherence to the "old ways" could no longer be sustained. Answers to mounting debt challenges and declining customer counts became increasingly elusive to industry icons, such as A&P, Winn Dixie, and a cast of others. Welcome to the boneyard.

One of the most notable examples of courageous counterintuitive thinking is the case of Ford Motor Company. As a result of the extraordinary consumer response, demand pressed Henry Ford to seek increasingly innovative solutions to increase production. The result was the advent of assembly line production. However, the repetitive tasks were uninspiring. Consequently, the company experienced inordinate quality problems and a confusingly high annual turnover rate of 370 percent, forcing Ford to hire 52,000 additional employees a year to compensate. Additionally, union strikes and worker absenteeism eroded profitability and created a significant decline in quality. These costly conditions triggered considerable discussion among leadership at Ford, with conventional solutions receiving most of the attention. After all, employee turnover is a familiar nail for the Hammerheads to address. However, Henry Ford made an extraordinarily counterintuitive decision. At great financial risk, he doubled wages. As a result, turnover dropped from 370 percent to 16 percent, while productivity improved as much as 70 percent. In addition, employee morale increased, and quality control issues were minimized. As an added bonus, higher wages also added to the Ford customer landscape, as workers were increasingly able to afford to purchase a Ford.

THINKING COUNTERINTUITIVELY

Effective leaders embrace the opportunity to challenge convention, regardless of whether the solutions apply or not. Ultimately, this counterintuitive thinking gives the leader a more complete toolbox. Then, it is just a matter of using the right tool for the right challenge. That, and a few million details.

Chapter 4

Turkeys in the Convocation— Inspiring Excellence

As it is often quipped, it is hard to soar like an eagle when you are surrounded by turkeys. In a world that measures results, eagles eat, turkeys get eaten. Exceptional organizations consist largely of eagles determined to thrive through excellence. They form a convocation that strives to produce extraordinary results—no matter how significant—and share a disdain for anything less. They compare their performance to best in class rather than industry average metrics. Mediocre organizations are predominantly a rafter of turkeys comforted into complacency. They have little competitive instinct, avoid challenges, and resist change. Exceptional organizations seek, attract, and easily retain eagles. And they deselect turkeys. Conversely, mediocre organizations attract turkeys and deselect eagles. And any eagles they are fortunate enough to land fly away quickly. Without scrutiny, neither recognizes the dynamic. In the end, eagles scream, and turkeys gobble. Eagles feast. Turkeys are feasted upon.

Notably, underperforming organizations hardly ever recognize mediocrity without existential performance declines. It has to hit the fan before anyone notices. These organizations fail to excel because they believe they consist of the finest in the industry. The absence of eagles has led them to the conclusion that their turkeys were, in fact, eagles. And they ultimately become the centerpiece of the feast, surrounded by potatoes, peas, and pies.

Responsible leaders hardly ever deliberately build an organization of turkeys. Every responsible leader constantly seeks the best and brightest talent available, and exceptional organizations institute practices that continually develop talent that drive excellence. However, mediocrity can easily consume any organization long before they recognize the issue.

Mediocrity begins with leadership and is sustained by all levels of management. Exceptional leaders demonstrate and promote, through behavior and expectations, relentless insistence upon excellence at all levels of the organization. Through their actions and accountabilities, every member of the organization understands the expectation to perform as eagles. Usually, these organizations enjoy remarkably low turnover rates, rarely struggle to find highly qualified talent, and reliably deliver on the business objectives.

Discordant organizations are not much different. Their leaders emphasize the importance of excellence and push the organization to deliver excellence. Yet they fail. This is largely due to a lack of discipline and ability to distinguish turkeys from eagles. Tone-deaf leaders inconsistently foster excellence through their own actions, and because they have little experience working with real eagles, they assume their turkeys are eagles.

Often compounding the mediocrity in many discordant organizations is myopic focus on distracting internal metrics that drive complacency. In the case of Kmart, internal metrics convinced leadership to believe all was going well. Even when alarms began to sound, the initial response was to essentially lower standards and redefine success.

Our most loyal customers are sticking with us. No reason to panic.

This response was exacerbated by denial. Kmart enjoyed enormous success for decades, and the glory years pervaded the leadership and operational ranks, reinforcing an increasing level of mediocrity they misinterpreted as excellence. They adjusted their metrics and performance expectations to be more consistent with mediocrity than excellence. Rather than focus on competitive metrics, they concentrated on metrics driven by a gradually shrinking core of top shoppers. Rather than focus on service excellence standards, they concentrated on squeezing more productivity out of an already stressed and underqualified workforce, making them a less attractive employment option to the retail labor pool. Then came Walmart. By the time Kmart's leadership recognized the existential threat driven by their mediocrity, it was too late. They were devoured.

Comfort fostered by complacency is a red flag for exceptional leaders and a security blanket for the tone-deaf. Exceptional leaders recognize the subtle signs of complacency and force their organizations to excel. Ineffective leaders ignore these signs or lower expectations and standards to a deeper level of mediocrity. Exceptional leaders notice when their organizations struggle to attract and retain exceptional talent and reemphasize their standards of excellence. Ineffective leaders ignore the signs or attribute the issue to market conditions, conveniently asserting that the quality of talent is suboptimal. Exceptional organizations rarely struggle with high turnover. Dysfunctional organizations invest inordinate resources in talent acquisition and frequently find that the only way to retain flight risks is by overcompensating them.

Another prevalent behavior among discordant organizations is the practice of overcompensating for mediocrity. This practice often focuses solutions on individuals rather than the organization, making exceptions and creating "workarounds" inconsistent with standard business practices. They excuse poor performance and tend to deflect responsibility. Like the poor carpenter, they blame their mistakes on the tools rather than themselves. Common indicators include the following:

- Inordinate number of individuals with "special assignments"
- Substantial number of individuals with "unique" reporting relationships
- Exceptional number of individuals with undefined roles
- Lots of "busy work" instead of "productive work"

- Frequent deflection ("weak economy," "shallow talent pool," "supplier failures," etc.) when discussing underperformance

Generally, the presence of any of these exceptions is a symptom of a culture of mediocrity. The result is often well-hidden discordance that makes creating harmony and identifying and resolving challenges increasingly difficult. Exceptions are noisy. Effective leaders quickly hear and address noisy exceptions. Tone-deaf leaders either fail to recognize the problems posed by the exceptions or refuse to responsibly address them.

While the workforce is at the core of excellence or mediocrity, discipline, process, and accountability are the key foundational elements. Eagles embrace and attack all. Turkeys meander.

At the leadership level, discipline is essential. Consistent behavior and communication relating to standards of excellence are imperatives that drive enterprise-wide success. Exceptional and consistent focus on vision and goals establishes and reinforces expectations at all levels. A disciplined and relentless focus on fundamentals ensures the importance of operational excellence at all levels. Exceptional leaders require exceptional discipline in fundamentals and require constant practice and refinement. Ineffective leaders tend to lack a disciplined approach to mission planning and frequently neglect fundamentals altogether, commonly resulting in failure at even the simplest tasks. At best, ineffective leaders emphasize fundamental excellence until the organization *gets it right*. Exceptional leaders emphasize fundamentals until they *no longer get it wrong*. With discipline and focus, operational excellence is easily achieved. Without it, mediocrity thrives.

As mission clarity is established, communicated, and reinforced at the leadership level, the process creates the road map that gets the organization there. Most high-performing organizations embrace the notion that process makes perfect, while most dysfunctional organizations consider the concept too corporate, bureaucratic, and unnecessary. These organizations fail to recognize the value of process because they achieve relative degrees of success on instinct and intellect. However, as competition, growth, and market conditions evolved, the absence of meaningful processes became glaring through missed deadlines, inefficient and overcomplicated practices, confusion, and high turnover. Eagles avoid these environments. Turkeys thrive in them.

Coupled with the process is accountability. Exceptional organizations establish accountabilities at all appropriate levels, giving everyone a clear and measurable understanding of what is expected and holding them accountable through consistent performance management practices. Exceptional organizations consist of people who demand accountability to understand exactly what defines success. Exceptional leaders consistently hold their teams accountable without exception. They openly celebrate success. These leaders measure performance multiple times during the course of a year and focus on the expected result each step of the way. They allow extenuating circumstances to be considered as possible influences on any shortfalls but factor those circumstances into performance management conversations regarding meeting the overall performance objectives. As a result, the organization maintains a singular focus on a clear objective and meaningful steps required to achieve it—collectively.

Mediocre organizations rarely apply accountability measures. Those that do inconsistently enforce the measures. As a result, the organization fails to excel because no consequences exist. This dynamic is not uncommon. Leaders who created the environment are not usually incompetent, lazy, or stupid. On the contrary, these leaders are often quite competent, driven, and intelligent. And they usually recognize the importance of accountability. However, they tend to be inconsistent and undisciplined when applying the concept enterprise-wide. They fail to celebrate success. They apply consequences on a case-by-case basis, focusing on personalities rather than performance. They adjust the objective—expected results—to accommodate mediocre performance rather than drive performance to the level of excellence demanded by the objective. They allow perfunctory performance management processes that are nothing more than ticking boxes once a year. They fail to recognize that one review at the end of the year is too late to correct any performance issues.

A common characteristic of dysfunctional organizations that struggle to enforce accountability is the tendency to confuse *account-*

ability with *blame*. The difference between the two has to do with objective perspective. Accountability is applied to functional performance. Blame is applied to the person. Ultimately, an individual is the focus of accountability. However, an organizational culture of accountability affects motivation at the personal level. An individual who works in an organization that objectively applies accountability practices tends to employ courage and initiative, recognizing accountability measures as *rewards* and *learning opportunities,* whereas an individual who works in an organization that subjectively applies accountabilities tends to operate conservatively for *fear of punishment*. Effective leaders create accountability processes that focus on fair, meaningful, and measurable results to motivate and empower excellence. Tone-deaf leaders use accountability as a weapon that tends to stifle creativity and courage and impedes course correction during difficult times.

To the astute leader, a flock of eagles is easily recognized. In addition to basic performance, the subtle characteristics of a convocation include the following:

- Harmony
- Enterprise-wide dissatisfaction with anything less than perfection
- Driven to win—even if they are playing checkers with their five-year-old child
- Low tolerance for failure and error
- Focus
- Discipline
- Practice fundamentals until they can no longer get them wrong
- The best talent wants to work there
- Turkeys do not last long
- Most turnover is limited to mediocre performers
- Competition is constantly trying to poach talent

The subtle characteristics of a rafter of turkeys are also easy to recognize. The characteristics include the following:

- Persistent mistakes at even the simplest tasks
- Indifferent about winning or losing
- High turnover, especially among high-performers
- Efforts to hire eagles driven by compensation and are pricey
- Any eagles they attract ultimately leave
- Failure to appreciate process
- Practice fundamentals until they get them right
- Unclear and inconsistently applied accountability practices
- Perfunctory performance management processes

Excellence attracts excellence, and mediocrity attracts mediocrity. Performance determines which exists. Demanding and reinforcing excellence through focused leadership, discipline, process, and accountability effectively enable an organization to soar with eagles rather than waddle with turkeys. Eagles feast. Turkeys are feasted on.

Chapter 5

The Carpenter Ant, the Fox, and the Dolphin—Work Hard and Smart

We usually imagine carpenter ants as industrious creatures, focusing their energy on cutting, lifting, and delivering a product. Foxes are generally known for being smart, constantly determining efficient ways of accomplishing an objective without expending more energy than they obtain through their efforts. Dolphins are commonly considered to be intelligent creatures who integrate hard work and intelligent work to meet their objectives.

Every organization ideally consists of people working diligently to fulfill a common mission. The distribution of duties and functional requirements, depending upon the nature of the organization or business, varies. Within each function exist those who work hard, those who work smart, and those who work hard and smart. High-functioning organizations tend to consist of people who strike a fine balance between working hard and working smart. Dysfunctional organizations do not. To paraphrase Tim Ferris, effective organizations focus on being productive instead of looking busy, while dysfunctional organizations consist of too many unproductive, busy people. Indeed, a productive symphony makes music, while a busy orchestra makes noise.

Ongoing enterprise improvements frequently identify and integrate opportunities to improve efficiency through process engineering. These improvements typically involve process improvements coupled with technological enhancements. The role of the industrial engineer, for example, greatly improves production through the invention and integration of tools that enhance production efficiency in a manufacturing environment. These process and technology enhancements vastly influence innovation, quality, and profitability. The "heavy lifting" often required is effectively minimized, creating harmony. Although many functions within an organization necessarily involve elbow grease and sweat, harmonious organizations efficiently distribute the energy to inspire an effective mix of hard work and smart work. The carpenter ants efficiently work through their tasks, the foxes constantly apply their wiles to process and infrastructure, and the dolphins ensure a proper balance of hard and smart work.

This harmony is commonly absent in low-performing or dysfunctional organizations. The inherent desire to productively fill forty hours a week often creates layers of efficient yet unproductive activities. As Peter Drucker wrote, "There is nothing so useless as doing efficiently that which should not be done at all."

Often the absence of harmony is a contributor to the adversity the organization finds itself facing. In some cases, adversity disrupts the harmony. Adversity often creates chaos among dysfunctional organizations, causing the ants to scurry, the foxes to revert to purely functional activity, and the dolphins to lose focus. This condition is easily overlooked, especially when an organization is in the throes of performance challenges, and is often an impediment to successful course correction. Time, short-term pressures, and myopic leadership obscure a holistic view of how the organization does what it does, allowing a pervasive imbalance to exist.

To evaluate how disharmony may be affecting adverse conditions, the first thing to do is identify easily unnoticed symptoms:

Are most tasks unnecessarily labor-intensive or cumbersome?
Is the workforce unnecessarily physically and mentally exhausted?
Has this perceived exhaustion become more prevalent than usual?

Are the "thinkers" in the organization spending an inordinate amount of time "rolling up their sleeves"? Has this changed over time?
Are people performing tasks expected of those one level below them?
Are vice presidents spending an inordinate amount of time doing the job of their director(s)?

Naturally, adversity prompts people to revert to survival mode. Negative trends often initiate reactionary behavior at all levels, beginning with top leadership. Notably, however, this reactionary leadership is usually an extension and amplification of one of the key causes of negative performance. To correct this, it is critical that leaders "take a beat." By honestly asking the following questions:

Why are we working so hard to do something so simple?
Are we overcomplicating what we do?
How much of our process is necessary? How much is sufficient? How has our drive to innovate made it harder to perform efficiently?
Why is our vice president of sales going on every cold call with our sales team?
Why is our vice president of software development spending so much time writing code rather than leading our programming team?
Is our current climate of exhaustion truly a result of our call for all hands on deck, or does it precede our current challenges?

Because these conditions are easily unrecognized, their contribution to the current challenges—whether as a precedent or as a circumstance—is rarely addressed. And as the severity of the circumstances increases, the ability to even recognize these conditions almost always becomes a second thought, at best. Effective leaders improve their chances of correcting negative performance by addressing these obscure conditions and decisively correcting the problematic behaviors with an open mind, clear communication, and demand for timely action.

Whether initiated by adversity or a catalyst of adversity, noisy organizations tend to neglect opportunities to address work effort imbalance.

MUSIC. NOT NOISE

As a result, the ants scurry, the foxes eat fewer calories than they burned to acquire those calories, and the dolphins find themselves swimming in circles. And the organization makes more noise than music.

Chapter 6

The Cube Farm—the Fastest Way to Lose Constituents Is to Lose Touch with Them

In many ways, societies across the world resemble the physical layout of an organization. Around the perimeter are offices occupied by qualified leaders who are responsible for establishing a vision, inspiring flawless execution, and delivering positive results. These denizens are in a stage of life that affords them unique luxuries and mentalities and represent a minor portion of the organization's workforce. In the center of the floor is a collection of cubicles, affectionately referred to as "cube farms," occupied by people responsible for executing and supporting decisions made in the offices. Their personal choices are more limited because of economics and various other factors that impact the office dwellers to a lesser degree, and they represent the majority of the organization's total workforce. The view the two have of life is commonly considerably different. Comparatively, society is dominated more by residents of the cube farm than the office dwellers. Yet most of the decisions that affect society reflect the attitudes and aspirations of people who do not experience the conditions life places on the majority of the population. Distressed organizations often fail to ask this simple question of relevance. Too often their solutions address the problems of the privileged.

During a conversation with the chairman of a large retailer, the topic of relevance arose. His reaction to the assertion that the decisions of his leaders had grown increasingly irrelevant was emphatic incredulity. He was also visibly insulted. So he joined me on a walk around the lower floors of the company. I pointed out to him that, like most companies, the ratio between offices and cubicles on any floor always skews heavily in favor of the cube farm. The offices are generally occupied by those making final decisions, while the cube farm is populated by those who support and execute those decisions. The lives of the two can be quite different. The priorities of life, while similar in many ways, differ significantly in others. Even executives who were not born to privilege run the risk of losing perspective on the everyday priorities of life.

"The world is just like this," I pointed out. "The core customer is more like the population in the cube farms of the corporate world. They live their lives practically and prudently. They pack their lunches rather than enjoy the local lunch spots. They calculate the cost of childcare to make sure they can even afford to go to work. Yet decisions are made in offices around the perimeter of the farm. How many of our decisions reflect the lives and mindsets of the cube farm population, and how many reflect the lives and mindsets of the office dwellers?"

He was lost in thought. The point was clearly made.

Most organizations proudly tout their "consumer-driven" approaches. Distressed organizations, when pressed to objectively and introspectively validate the assertion, realize that this is rhetoric rather than reality. Distressed organizations commonly dictate *to*, rather than empathize *with*, their consumers.

In the case of this retailer, the disconnect was palpable. As a retailer with a long and prosperous history, the office dwellers felt strongly that their customers prioritized quality over value. In a specific instance, the head of produce passionately believed in the company's insistence on providing only the highest quality apples. The qualities of these apples included uniform color and notably larger sizes. These qualities also came with a price, often as much as twice as much as the major competitors were asking for their apples. And those competitors were selling more apples.

"Sure" was the response. "But their apples are inferior. They aren't perfectly colored and are small. Our customers want big, beautiful apples and are willing to spend more."

This was true, but it only reflected the requirements of a customer base that lived in the offices. The market, however, reflected the requirements of the cube farm. They appreciated and expected quality, just like everyone else. But quality comes with a price that just fails to balance out for them. The produce head felt that the solution was to communicate the quality difference to make the consumer understand why his apples were better. If he did a better job of marketing his quality superiority, the consumer would be convinced that his apples were better for them. It did not work. The working mother of three knew that her children would never eat an entire apple that big (waste) and could not care less about how evenly colored it was, focused primarily on affordably giving her children something healthy that they would eat. If they happened to be huge and look pretty as well, so be it. But first things first.

This scenario is common among most companies in distress. In most cases, these companies choose to double down on what they firmly believe is a key point of differentiation. They fail to realize that their strategy is relevant, but only to people like them. The rest of the consumer base just feels like "they really don't get me."

This phenomenon does not occur because the leaders are incompetent or malicious. In most cases, the decision-makers are accomplished, capable, and truly feel they are doing things that the consumer desires. However, their perspective skews their vision. After years of tireless work to maintain competitiveness, these decision-makers lose their ability to empathize. They think *for* the consumer rather than *with* the consumer. They become tone-deaf. Companies in distress stopped challenging their own thinking with reality-driven questions that often also challenge their own humility.

Is this decision one that will resonate with people in the cube farm? Is my personal good fortune blinding me to the realities of general society?

Will a struggling family appreciate this big, beautiful apple that costs much more? Or will they just imagine that their seven-year-old is going to enjoy the smaller, less perfect-looking, but more affordable apple just as much?

This introspection is almost always absent in dysfunctional organizations. It is not the only cause of downturns. It is a considerable contributor. The complicating issue is that the errant decisions are commonly only the tip of the iceberg. A choice that turns out to be irrelevant to the consumer base can be quickly corrected. However, the organizational culture that fuels the choice prevents recognition and empathy essential to even identify such flawed thinking. As such, leaders resort to solutions that fall on deaf ears. To think that the answer is to explain why you are worth more to a consumer who is only hearing that you don't "get them" is like trying to pluck a piccolo. It just does not work.

The underlying culture of irrelevant thinking is difficult to correct, primarily because it is almost impossible to diagnose. Too much is personally and professionally invested in a direction that suggests the possibility of flawed thinking. More importantly, the mentality of most office dwellers is easily prone to a perspective that fails to match that of a broader society. Of course, the decisions do resonate among like thinkers. However, the universe of like-thinking people is a considerably small portion of the overall consumer base. Certainly, some business models exist on exclusivity, which means that they remain relevant to a narrow and focused base that shares their views on the value proposition. These businesses understand their customers because they are one and the same. As long as the narrow customer base supports the business requirements, this works. Few businesses survive on such a model, though. The necessity of remaining relevant to diverse consumer bases requires diverse thinking, decision-making, and empathetic perspectives. If your business landscape consists of office dwellers, decisions from the office dweller perspective are likely appropriate. If the business landscape is more diverse or is more populated by the cube farm, diverse perspectives are necessary. Most importantly, empathy is essential. More importantly, understanding that empathy is thinking and feeling *with* the consumer rather than *for* the consumer is the key.

Such myopia is usually developed innocently. It is just human nature to see the rest of the world through our own lens. Organizations that address the issue quickly are those with leaders who recognize the possibility that their choices could be skewed and enable diverse perspectives with processes that demand diverse input to encourage decisions that ensure relevance. Doing so is rarely simple or easy. Abandoning myopic thinking, especially when it worked for years, is frightening and unlikely to be considered. Leaders who effectively address office dweller myopia tend to embrace a few common practices.

- Think "with" not "for."
- Evolve with your customer.
- Remember that the world is bigger than you.
- Accept that times change. What worked before doesn't necessarily work today.
- Ignore self-validating information.
- Surround yourself with cube farm thinkers.

The most difficult thing to do is accept the possibility that we could even remotely be biased by our own perspectives. Most people want to believe that they understand people, their markets, and their customers. Most people genuinely insist that they know what matters to their customers and work tirelessly to make those customers happy. To consider otherwise is to acknowledge personal flaws. Such acknowledgment is rare. Get over it.

Organizations with long histories are exceptionally prone to stagnancy in evolving times. A history of success reassures them that their decisions will work. Failure to recognize the evolution of consumer requirements is an easy trap into which to fall. The reality is that consumer bases evolve. Technology has accelerated this evolution, placing control firmly in the hands of the consumer by expanding their choices. That evolution demands self-reflection to ensure that decision-making reflects the cube farm. Evolve or die.

Another dangerous trap is relying on tailored data that validate potentially faulty thinking driven by biased perspectives. The explosion of corporate insistence on data-driven decision-making has generally improved performance exponentially. However, good tools are sometimes used wrongly. Wrongly used data becomes a destructive weapon rather than a productive tool. This is especially prevalent among distressed companies. These companies commonly find themselves perplexed by data that support choices but are disputed by the performance data. When it comes to consumer-facing choices, this problem is exacerbated by the slow return of performance data (assuming they even exist). Almost all companies under duress share the *selective data syndrome*. These selective data are tailored by the need to validate the decisions. As performance begins to decline, these tailored data continue to support the original decision, thus guiding leaders to look elsewhere for solutions. Effective leaders challenge the potential existence of inherent bias in data that both drive decisions and measure their performance. The best data are bias-free data.

Finally, avoiding the pitfalls of shortsighted leadership requires diverse thinking that inspires leaders to sincerely demand the perspective of the cube farm. Most leaders genuinely believe that they understand the consumer perspective, but those who are at the helm of sinking ships refuse to acknowledge the likelihood that they are not as empathetic as they believe themselves to be. The most effective leaders continually push themselves to think diversely but surround themselves with people reflecting the diverse mentality as insurance. These people are necessarily courageous and candid.

The most effective organizations encourage leadership from every chair, whether in an office or a cubicle. The most effective organizations consist of leaders who take genuine action to ensure that truly diverse thinking is applied to consumer-facing decisions through humility, nimbleness that allows them to evolve quickly, insistence on sound and unbiased information, and surrounding themselves with perspectives that ensure that the proper perspective is infused in every decision. Harmonious companies have such a culture. Discordant companies do not.

Chapter 7

This Is What We Do—Selling Chicken and Cheerios

A tree that stops growing starts dying. Companies evolve, or they die. This necessary and ongoing evolutionary process applies to the overall organization, as well as the functions, systems, processes, and people within. The pressures of competition and relevance force business leaders to find smarter, faster, compelling ways to be who they are and do what they do. A common characteristic of struggling organizations is a gradual deviation from who they are and what they do as pressures mount. As a complete unit, as well as its parts, many organizations find it difficult to recognize their original selves. Something changed, and it took them off course. They became unrecognizable. They stopped being who they were established to be. They stopped doing what they do.

Externally, the evolving consumer appreciates businesses that evolve with them. Their hunger for new and exciting products and services drives innovation in companies. The growth and influence of technological advances create a new platform from which innovative products and services are launched and enhanced. The demands of emerging generations, driven by shorter attention spans, diverse value sets, adventurous mentalities, and simple boredom, have been an even more significant impetus for innovation. Of course, boredom and demands for something new are not mutually exclusive. In a demand-driven society, we must make what people will buy.

Both of these factors influence the competitive pace in dramatic and exciting ways.

Estée Lauder serves as an excellent example of how diligent focus on core DNA at the portfolio and brand levels leads to sustainable success. Demand for growth and innovation constantly occupy the attention of leaders throughout the organization. Product and service innovation and portfolio growth through sensible but dynamic acquisition are essential to sustaining its position as an industry leader. Importantly, decision-making within the company always focuses on ensuring consistency with the DNA of the individual brands, as well as that of the portfolio.

> *Is this product consistent with our brand?*
> *Does this campaign clearly reflect who we are and what we are to our customers?*
> *Does this acquisition target complement our portfolio DNA? Positionally? Operationally?*

The result of this focus is an impressive track record of growth—in good times and bad. At the brand level, decisions never confuse their customers. Whether these decisions involve innovation or operation, both the retail customer and the end user are always clear about who the brand is. At the operational level, this focus ensures that the processes of creating, manufacturing, and distributing the product are consistent at all levels and in each market they serve. For example, one of the key criteria for viable acquisition targets is consistency with the portfolio's distribution model. No matter how attractive the target might be, it must either fit into the current distribution model or can be efficiently integrated into the existing distribution model. In each case, they stay true to who they are, what they do, and how they do it.

General Motors is an example of how demand for growth threatened the company due to increased operational obscurity, but nimble and thoughtful leadership capitalized on a new opportunity in a familiar vertical.

THIS IS WHAT WE DO

In the early 2000s, the GMAC financing arm became the company's leading source of profit, while the core competency—making and selling cars and trucks—was struggling in an intensely competitive market. Holistically, the company was not performing to its potential because valuable resources were diluted. The car company was not receiving the necessary focus to compete successfully, and the finance company was undervalued because of the sluggish performance driven by the car company.

Wisely, management decided to spin the finance arm off. The result was to refocus on the two units independently. The finance arm became more accurately valued, and the automobile business returned as a more pure, focused player in the automobile industry.

And, of course, there is Amazon, which transformed itself from an online bookstore to the largest retailer on earth. Realizing their capabilities as an online retailer, they expanded their offering while sticking with who they are, what they do, and how they do it. As a result, even while integrating data analysis and advertising into their revenue stream, they leveraged the platform's capabilities, supply and logistics infrastructure, and merchandising talents without deviating from who they are.

Lack of disciplined focus almost always results in costly dysfunction. McDonald's experienced innovation-driven pains as it pursued new ways to expand market penetration through the introduction of its "Made for You" concept. The innovative idea came at the expense of efficiency and consistency—its best-known qualities. Every burger and batch of fries is supposed to be made exactly the same way, which keeps its food fast, consistent, and cheap. Blinded by a drive to innovate, leadership failed to recognize how making significant changes to its food preparation would hinder its ability to maintain speed and keep costs down. Customers just wanted a decent burger that was inexpensive and fast.

Believing customers wanted more customized orders, the head of the US division overhauled the company's entire food preparation system to introduce the concept. The initiative involved burgers cooked to order with freshly toasted buns. In addition to costly retooling, the program drastically extended wait times. This took the "fast" out of "fast food." Ultimately, although well-intentioned, the program failed. It was inconsistent with who they are, what they do, and how they do it. The billion-dollar diversion negatively impacted sales, as well as the company's stock value.

While the appetite for innovation is a prominent, self-created diversion, many external factors also distract organizations from their core competence. Pressures from the investment community and corporate boards for companies to keep pace with the rapidly evolving competitive landscape require businesses to address the necessity of evolution. These pressures are relentless and impatient. Often subtle, these pressures manifest themselves through erratic leadership and decision-making.

Another driver of constant evolution is boredom. The fact is that companies are comprised of people. People want to grow. Just as consumers seek innovation, so do employees. From the line to leadership, people within companies are curious about innovating what they do and how they do it. This curiosity has led to some of the most remarkable advancements in history and will be responsible for the many to come. The dreamers will make life better. Most of the time.

Collectively, these external and internal variables often lead companies down paths that result in confusion. This confusion frequently translates into poor results. Aggressive growth through diversity and enhancement easily distracts operations from their primary purpose. Because growth is often comfortable and exciting, it is easy for people to deviate from the reason they are there, what they do, and how they do it. Carpenters build things; they do not just hammer nails.

European grocery chains Tesco and Sainsbury experienced divergent results from their approaches to challenges. Sainsbury embarked on an aggressive strategy that added new lines of business through acquisitions of retail chains in Egypt and Texas. Tesco, on the other hand, decided not to stray far from its core business. Instead, it added new products and services—such as eyeglasses and coffee shops in its existing stores. For the next ten years, Tesco's stock price grew 291 percent, while Sainsbury's stock only grew 38 percent.

THIS IS WHAT WE DO

Tesco Chairman Lord Ian McLauren asserted, "We knew we were a supermarket and only invested in things that we could prove our customers really wanted."

In the face of adversity, organizations can easily identify significant diversions from their core purpose. Astute leaders quickly identify activities that are inconsistent with the core mission and competencies, redirect resources to ensure greater focus on the core purpose, and minimize distractions associated with anything inconsistent with the core mission. However, operational models are arguably the most susceptible to core DNA diversion and pose a much greater threat. While larger strategic decisions that divert from the core competency can be damaging, they are more easily corrected than those that occur at the operational level. Many struggling organizations wake to find themselves in a boiling pot but have created an operational model through time that makes it nearly impossible to climb out or douse the flame. Perhaps one of the most notable cases of this exists in an entire industry.

For generations, the supermarket industry existed on a simple model and enjoyed extraordinary prosperity. In the early days, the mantra was simple—"pile it high and watch it fly." The best of the breed made sure that they provided products that their customers wanted at a fair price and backed the offering with excellent customer service. The simple model encouraged them to expand their footprint, drive new product and retail atmosphere innovation, and explore new ways to maximize margin. Enter an evolving competitor and consumer landscape that quickly wrenched control from the individual retailer. New formats, such as club, mass, and e-commerce, quickly commoditized the business by emphasizing price and convenience. Quickly, others joined in, creating a channel blur that will forever be the norm. Today, consumers can find many of the same products at any of a number of nontraditional retailers. This expanded freedom of choice firmly puts the consumer in control. However, many traditional grocers failed to evolve.

At the core of their inability to evolve is a merchandising model that grew over many years, shifting internally from sales to profit margin. Indeed, many merchandising groups in today's grocers, and most of those who have disappeared, allowed margin demands to supersede sales and transaction metrics. A component of this focus was the growth in the chasm between revenue lines—specifically sales and income. Over time, competitive challenges began to force merchants to seek new ways to protect margin performance. The path of least resistance was to "margin up" and increase merchandising income. At the core, neither of these had anything to do with simply selling chicken and Cheerios. Merchandising leadership became hypnotized by margin demands. Over time, the diversion became destructive.

As margin pressures intensified, the least adaptive merchants simply increased prices, while the more evolved merchants developed new pricing strategies that focused on more controlled pricing strategies. While some retailers have implemented effective pricing strategies that maximized margin without diminishing sales and customer counts, more failed.

Even more pervasive is the evolution of the merchandising income model. During boom times, the retailer and manufacturer partnership allowed innovative market approaches that manufacturers found worthy of significant investment beyond traditional retail practice. However, manufacturers' priorities begin at home. As the landscape evolved and performance pressures intensified, the manufacturing community reassessed its retail investments. After all, any business investment serves two purposes—make me money or save me money. This focus resulted in shifts in the retail model that quickly reduced the merchandising income pad. Separate buckets for pure merchandising income declined, and the manufacturer's "ask" for the desired investment increased. While this consumed the bulk of merchandising attention, the focus on selling chicken and Cheerios diminished.

Unfortunately, the model was ingrained in the merchant's DNA through years of practice. The merchandising model became and continues to be, for many, about margin rather than profitably selling chicken and Cheerios to as many people as possible. Perhaps the most influential component of the antiquated model has to do with personal compensation. As the model evolved, bonuses and performance evaluations increasingly relied more on merchandising income than on sales and market share growth. Because merchandising income tends to be somewhat more controllable, distressed merchandising organizations were reluctant to shift their focus back to simply selling chicken and Cheerios. Continued poor results were easily deflected, and bonuses continued to reflect margin performance above other metrics. It did not work. Conversely, had the focus remained on ways to sell products to consumers through innovative wallet share initiatives and less on superficial tactics, the challenges may have been minimized.

Another industry that suffered focus diversion is news media. The inception of the twenty-four-hour news format resoundingly illustrates how a seemingly breakthrough concept can obscure focus on the core purpose. Throughout history, the role of the media has grown increasingly significant in societies around the world. As it evolved through demand and innovation, the core purpose grew meaningfully important and influential, helping shape nations and influence growth. At the core, the purpose was universally clear—inform, educate, and entertain. As the industry grew increasingly relevant to day-to-day life, its own evolution included an expansion into editorial, as well as pure informational content. With technology came new opportunities to reach the masses more efficiently. Finally, the commercial opportunities attracted significant attention. As a result, the competitive media landscape grew rapidly and exponentially.

The competitive boom and technology advancements fueled the onset of the twenty-four-hour news cycle. On June 1, 1980, CNN launched the news version of the Cold War "Space Race," kicking off a worldwide industry trend that inspired Fox and MSNBC to quickly follow after the inarguable success enjoyed from coverage of the Gulf War in 1991. Viewers were glued to screens. Advertisers noticed. The floodgates were blasted off their hinges. After Fox and MSNBC joined the fray, twenty-four-hour news channels expanded worldwide in nations including Australia, France, Germany, Pakistan, Russia, and more. With the Internet, accessibility to viewers drove innovative media leaders to quickly identify ways to leverage the new frontier, and new generations of information seekers flocked to their new screens.

Money and myopia, however, changed the media landscape. To compete for revenue, media organizations found themselves constantly looking for new differentiation points. And then there is the format itself. The twenty-four-hour cycle meant that the industry had to develop content to fit the format—even if real news did not exist. The economics of the media industry created considerable pressure for its leaders to provide measurable value to its internal and external stakeholders. Professional competitiveness drove them to focus on one another, often at the expense of the reader, listener, or viewer. Thus began a pattern that distorted the core purpose of conventional media sources. The pure focus on informing, educating, and entertaining became increasingly blurry.

This distorted perspective created a media landscape that has tailored the facts to their selected ideologies driven by their chosen core audiences. They choose what to report, what not to report, and how to report the pure information. They entrench themselves as right-wing and left-wing media. The demands of the format have created platforms predominantly consisting of opinion panels and talking heads. As a result, the media industry we have today creates as much confusion as it does understanding and is less trustworthy than ever before. The importance and value of the media to global societies is unquestionable. However, the evolution of the industry has eroded credibility because, on the whole, objectivity has become obscured. The evolution has distorted the industry's core purpose—to inform, to educate, and to entertain. Instead, many outlets present subjective ideologies and superficial sensationalism. The consumer has to work harder to know what is happening in the world.

Diversion from core organizational purpose also occurs when seemingly natural additions to the core offering become prominent, thus distracting focus and investment. Just because your new prize bulldog can jump over a low fence does not mean that it is a prize jumper that you should enter a horse jumping competition. Heavy investment in a jumping bulldog only wastes your time and annoys the dog. Diverse offerings can be of value. However, misplaced focus can be costly. These diversions tend to be exceptionally evident among organizations struggling to overcome adversity, largely because they are latent. With relentless focus on the primary objective, diversion is less likely.

Former US Secretary of State and Chairman of the Joint Chiefs of Staff Colin Powell put it best when he said that m*ission clarity* is critical to success. Establishing this clarity at the global and micro levels is essential. Globally, what the organization does—what it really does—must be spoken, written, and shared. Each group within the organization must fight through the myopia to find clarity on two levels—(1) the functional mission and (2) how that functional mission directly interacts with other functions to serve the organizational mission.

One of the most common characteristics among almost every dysfunctional organization is the prevalence of individuals doing the job of the person one level below them. This is one of the most disruptive phenomena an organization can experience. The C-suite focuses too much of its energy on subordinate tasks. Vice presidents spend inordinate energy doing what their directors should be doing. Directors spend the majority of their time doing the manager's job. Not to be confused with micromanaging, this common phenomenon creates discord at all levels. It manifests in ways that result in leadership voids at a critical point in the life of the organization.

Whether the phenomenon is a symptom or a cause of adversity varies from one case to the other. This applies in the most innocuous corners of any organization. From the corner office to the proverbial mail room, focus on the core purpose is essential. Diversion is disruptive. In the case of the analytics group of a global retailer, exciting advances in technological enablers and growing internal appreciation for information and insights ignited a passion within the group that resulted in innovative investments and approaches to how data could be used to define the past and predict the future. At times, though, the process of collecting and analyzing the data became more about the data and analytics. Leaders within the organization sometimes struggled to determine how these insights could be used to inspire ways to sell more chicken and Cheerios. The simple solution was to collectively reaffirm the global purpose of the group and reaffirm the message from time to time. The result was the global inclusion of the group's work into tactical and strategic decision-making.

> *We have invested in the best mathematicians and data analysts. We have supplied them with the most innovative tools to enable them to create impressive algorithms and insights to keep us competitive. But is this investment helping us sell more chicken and Cheerios? Actually, this data bore me. How I can use them to make or save more money is what excites me!*
>
> *These insights are impressive, and the PowerPoint slides are engaging, but what is the message?*
>
> *The charts, formulas, and insights are impressive. But what are they saying? It's like they are speaking a different language. How do we translate this so that store-level managers and merchandisers can use it to sell more products? We're merchants, not scientists.*

Each group within the organization must fight through myopia and overzealous innovation to ensure clarity at both the corporate and functional levels. Certainly, intellectual and practical diversification is helpful and often necessary to seed sustainable growth. However, the practical and often unforeseen impact demands scrutiny. The importance of focusing on selling chicken and Cheerios during diverse change is critical. Without the critical focus on the core purpose of the organization, as well as the totality of its functions, strategic and tactical missteps occur as this purpose becomes gradually obscured. Ultimately, the purpose of the organization is to sell chicken and Cheerios. Effective leaders always remember this. Tone-deaf leaders do not.

Chapter 8

Flat Squirrels—Lead. Follow. Or Get Out of the Way!

Highways are lined with flat squirrels who could not make up their minds. The list of failed organizations that were paralyzed by indecision is long. Adverse conditions can be jolting, often inducing early onset paralysis among decision-makers. This paralysis is especially evident among organizations that struggle to combat adverse conditions. Whether the cause, symptom, or both, intellectual paralysis is a key impediment in the battle. This paralysis is a constant feature of struggling companies.

Ted Turner was known to display a plaque in his outer office that read, "Lead. Follow. Or get out of the way!" The phrase emphasizes the importance of decisive and prompt ownership of leadership responsibilities. Indeed, winners are quick to lean into their responsibilities as leaders. Decisive action, clear communication, and measurable plans produce music through sound leadership and resolute execution. Leaders lead. Followers follow. Effective leaders are usually the first voice in the room, clarifying the problem, focusing their energy on informed solutions, and informing and inspiring others to execute.

Confusion occurs when people fail to step into one of these roles. Compounding this confusion is an abundance of individuals who do step into these roles but are tone-deaf. In distressed organizations, chaos is a result of this failure. Hand-wringing, finger-pointing, indecision, and costly mistakes are a few of the many consequences of organizations consisting of designated leaders who fail to assertively own their obligations. Moreover, the chaos results in numerous people who get in the way of necessary progress. When asked "who is responsible," respondents often share witless stares with one another. They are roadkill without realizing it.

Senior executives are responsible for making decisions, and the associated risks and rewards are typically calculated. Under adverse conditions, decision-making becomes a quick victim. Any decision has the potential of going wrong as the many million details make themselves known. More destructive, however, is the lack of decision—inaction—or, more commonly, slow decision-making. Indecision is common among distressed organizations and is caused by a multitude of factors. Any of these factors directly create noise rather than music. Among these factors are denial, fear, discordant decision-making processes complicated by overly complicated organizational structure, and overthinking the problem and the solutions.

Companies that have failed often knew what was happening but chose not to do much about it. Sometimes, they take action, but often their actions are too little too late. They are ultimately flattened by indecision.

Fear is personal. And it is paralyzing. Especially during adverse times, a palpable absence of courageous thinkers is obvious. No one is prepared to risk personal security by making a decision. Instead, they tend to wait for someone else to make the decision for them, thereby reducing personal risk. Other times, this fear prevents decision-makers from challenging the status quo to ask the tough questions. Effective leaders lead with selfless courage. Tone-deaf leaders try to pass the baton.

Sheer size is another key impediment to effective decision-making. The larger the organization, the more crucial an efficient decision-making process becomes. Because of size, bureaucratic barriers create multiple choke points that prevent decisions and relative action. Each layer within an organization impedes decisive action, resulting in a slow reaction to changing conditions. Conversely, successful leaders draw a clear line from each dot along the decision line to the common destination—action.

Kodak is one of the most often cited companies as an example of a company that failed due to slow decision-making. Another is Blockbuster. In the face of competition from emerging DVD-by-mail services like Netflix and the shift to digital streaming, Blockbuster was hesitant to shift its business model. The company was slow to recognize the potential of online streaming and delayed in developing a digital platform to compete with Netflix. Blockbuster's reluctance to pivot toward the digital era ultimately led to its downfall, with most of its stores closing and the company filing for bankruptcy in 2010.

Analysis paralysis is a popular vernacular for overthinking. Successful leaders insist on collecting and analyzing information to ensure sound decision-making. A clear understanding of all factors influencing current business conditions is essential. Distressed organizations often find themselves paralyzed by the process, requiring information that fully explains the conditions and perfectly defines the appropriate course of action. This demand for perfection is unrealistic. Because the information rarely meets the requirement, decisions become the victims. This requirement is actually very real and is prevalent among the more detail-oriented and analytic people.

Most importantly, information must be addressed very methodically. *What? So what? Now what?* This approach to analytics is crucial to preventing analysis paralysis. Once accurate data are collected, an analysis must use the facts as a tool toward actionability. The *what* of information has to do with the facts. Many organizations get stuck at this level. The *so what* is difficult but creates the insights derived from the information. *Now what* is the pot of gold. This elusive stage of analytics focuses on the implied actions of the information and insights.

Former US Secretary of State and Chairman of the Joint Chiefs, Colin Powell, had a rule of thumb about making tough decisions. Universally known as the "40–70 Rule," Powell said that every time you face a tough decision, you should have no less than 40 percent and no more than 70 percent of the information you need to make the decision. If you make a decision with less than 40 percent of the information you need, you are shooting from the hip, and you will make too many mistakes. Additionally, if you get more than 70 percent of the information you need to make the decision, then the opportunity has usually passed, and someone else has beaten you to the punch. A key element that supports Powell's rule is the notion that intuition is what separates great leaders from the average ones. However, organizations beset by analysis paralysis often ignore the value of instinct. Powell's rule insists on integrating the right mix of instinct and information to make prompt and effective decisions. Prompt and informed decisions beget action.

Often, distressed organizations compound analysis paralysis by asking the wrong questions. The movie *Finding Forrester* contains a moment that poignantly illustrates this common behavior. The movie is about a man named William Forrester, an author who published one great novel and then became a recluse living in New York, and Jamal Wallace, an unlikely teenage savant who becomes Forrester's friend. Early in their relationship, Forrester asks Jamal to stir his soup so a skin will not form. At one point over dinner, Jamal asks why the soup his mother makes at home does not thicken like the kind Forrester makes. Forrester says it is the milk. Then Jamal asks the novelist why he is so reclusive, and Forrester says, "That's not exactly a soup question." The object of a question is to find information that matters to us, Forrester says, and no one else. A soup question yields an answer that will benefit the objective. In the first instance, Jamal learns something about various ways to make soup. This is to his benefit. It increases his knowledge. But as to the second question, Forrester points out that knowing intimate details of his life is not a benefit to Jamal. All questions are informative. Soup questions are actionable. Many organizations fall into this trap, especially when attempting to illustrate existing challenges. In distressed organizations, proportionately few of the questions are soup questions.

FLAT SQUIRRELS

Effective approaches to discordant decision-making are always unique to the organization. However, prescriptive measures do apply, regardless of unique factors. These include the following:

- Clearly define the objective of the decision.
- Focus on the soup questions.
- Gather enough information that will facilitate informed decisions.
- Identify alternatives to reduce "one size fits all" solutions.
- Establish success metrics and processes.
- Take Action.
- Measure.

Decision-making is an ongoing responsibility of any leader. Invariably, some decisions will work while others will fail. The most important thing is that decisions are made—with information, instinct, and focus on measurable action. Without this resolve, joining the ranks of flat squirrels is inevitable.

Chapter 9

Steak before Sizzle— Maslow Had a Point

In his Hierarchy of Needs model, psychologist Abraham Maslow delineates the steps humans travel to, as he terms it, "self-actualization." At the foundation of the hierarchy, basic needs must be satisfied, followed by safety needs, belongingness, and then esteem before attaining self-actualization. The approach applies in any setting involving people. The hierarchy easily translates into a "relationship model" that can apply to an employer and its employees, organizations and their customers, organizations and their partners, and organizations and their external stakeholders. Replacing "self-actualization" with "trust" at the pinnacle establishes a road map to solidifying relationships and identifying faults. With each constituency, the levels are defined the same but are adjusted according to personally relevant motivators. Commonly, discordant organizations share a progressive pattern of focusing more on the higher levels of the hierarchy, destructively forsaking the necessary basic levels. This is focusing on the sizzle rather than the steak.

For example, the basic need for employees is a job that enables them to support themselves, their families, and their lifestyles. They work to live rather than live to work. The safety need involves simple safety concerns, as well as a sense of job security. The belongingness need involves an employee's desire to be a part of something bigger than him or herself. This includes a sense of "family," as well as a meaningful role in society at large. The esteem level involves respect. Employees desire a place to work that respects them, and they respect their employers. If these levels are satisfied, the employee trusts the organization. Productivity tends to be enhanced, and morale is often high. Effective organizations strike a harmonious balance between the hierarchy levels of their employees, never losing sight of the basic needs—secure jobs paying a livable wage—and the higher-level needs. This effective culture typically results in a highly efficient, harmonious, and loyal workforce. In the face of inevitable adversity, these organizations typically respond quickly, decisively, harmoniously, and effectively. Results tend to be positive. Turnover tends to be minimal. Performance tends to be optimal. They make music.

Conversely, struggling organizations commonly exhibit an inequitable focus on the higher, more superficial needs—the sizzle—distracting them from ensuring a necessary consistent focus on the fundamentals—the steak. This distraction is often both a symptom and a cause of adversity. Most importantly, it is an entirely controllable condition, typically attributed to but hardly ever created by external forces.

In the employment model, many organizations are consistently recognized for their appealing employment practices. Varying by industry and workforce composition, longevity standards have evolved through the years as populations—people—have evolved. Rare is the long-standing model that culminates in retirement and a gold watch after a lifetime of service to one company. Today, people change jobs frequently and quickly. This change amplifies the role of the various needs to them. Earlier models relied on basic needs—a fair wage for a fair day's work. Security that the organization is going to be around forever. Familial cultures that integrated nuclear families with work families. Occasional tokens of esteem. With luck…a gold watch.

Today, while tenure statistics are varied, most sources conclude that today's workforce has no intention of remaining with one company forever. This is largely due to increased focus on the higher needs levels. No longer is a fair wage and job security enough to build long-standing trust. Today's workforce requires constant growth—

both professionally and personally—to be satisfied, meaning that continued growth initiatives are imperative to any human capital model.

Most notably, mutual respect plays an increasingly important role in talent retention, particularly when it comes to eagles. More than ever, today's labor pools must feel respected and must respect current leadership. And they are less patient because they have more options.

Hilton is consistently cited as one of the most successful when it comes to employee engagement. Their employment model addresses each of the needs levels to varying degrees of effectiveness. However, their credible emphasis on belongingness and esteem through their well-documented immersion program has engendered strong engagement among most levels of the organization. Consequently, Hilton consistently ranks high among organizations people want to work for.

A benchmark example of striking a manageable balance between steak and sizzle at the employee level is Google. The global tech leader has set the tone for many of the perks and benefits start-ups are now known for. Free meals, employee trips and parties, financial bonuses, open presentations by high-level executives, gyms, a dog-friendly environment, and many other cultural attributes illustrate a sensible focus on balance between the needs levels of employees. This balance has ensured a culture of inspiring, driven, talented, and generally fulfilled employees who contribute to the mission. The company has also recognized the importance of cultural adaptation, establishing systems and processes that enable it to reinvent itself through growth, adversity, and industry evolution. Of course, no company is immune to growing pains. Google has experienced the adversity associated with its growth, as well as the growth of the industry. However, Google continues to focus on striking a balance between steak (basic needs, employees' needs) and sizzle (belongingness, esteem) despite constant internal and external evolution. As a result, employee metrics (stellar reviews for pay/perks/advancement, talent retention, premium talent acquisition, productivity, customer satisfaction, etc.) continually reflect a balanced culture.

Unique to talent acquisition and retention, consequences of leadership that struggle to compel confidence are limited. Unlike customers and stakeholders, who can simply stop buying or investing if they lose confidence in leadership competence, employees must make life-impacting decisions if they lose confidence. As their options have increased exponentially, employees—particularly eagles—are quicker to consider leaving rather than staying. Effective leaders recognize the increased importance of mutual esteem in attracting and retaining eagles but address these higher-level needs without overlooking the basic needs. Often, dysfunctional organizations forsake the steak for sizzle.

The global response to the COVID-19 pandemic illustrates a distinct dichotomy of leadership focus on the needs hierarchy. Many countries faced the public health and economic realities of the crisis soberly, quickly, and responsibly. Most of those leaders, with a relentless focus on identifying, containing, and controlling the impact of the disease on their citizens, responded more quickly than some of the more powerful leaders around the globe. They focused on the basic needs of their constituents. They recognized that the virus had become an existential threat at the most individual levels. They focused their actions on saving lives. They kept their attention on the steak. As a result of their focus on the steak, these leaders efficiently protected their citizens.

The basic need was survival. The pandemic posed a science-supported existential threat to that need. Next on the hierarchy was safety. The outbreak threatened the sense of security at both physical and economic levels. Following safety was belongingness. Properly handled, the ideal pandemic action plan would address the holistic needs of the nation, not to mention the world. By emphasizing the totality of the threat and the shared impacts, the ideal plan would unite citizens to endure sacrifice and defeat the enemy as one. The next level on the hierarchy of needs is esteem. The ideal plan would recognize the collective actions of the warriors in the battle, as well as the fruits of their individual sacrifices. Finally, the pinnacle of the hierarchy is self-actualization. To paraphrase Maslow, this level could be redefined as trust. Especially when facing existential threats, trust in leadership is earned and crucial. Simply demanding trust from people when their lives and livelihoods are in peril without earning it by satisfying the other needs levels does not work.

United States leaders focused the bulk of their attention and resources on the sizzle, insisting that citizens simply trust their judgment. From the Oval Office to senior congressional leaders to local leaders to a gaggle of influencers, the pandemic was met with dismissal and denial. Minimization of the threat to the basic need—survival—created chaos and doubt. Most of the meaningful action bypassed the basic and safety needs, instead focusing on belongingness that predominantly impressed a subculture of sycophants, dishonoring the concept of *e pluribus unum*.

As the realities became more evident, the *sizzle syndrome* intensified. Leaders compounded dismissal and denial with a focus on deflection and distraction. Racist branding—"China Flu," "Kung Flu"—intensified the heat on the skillet, allowing deniers to direct attention to a bogeyman behind the crisis. Intense sizzle created a massive ideological chasm. Sizzle intensity created distrust in the expectedly trustworthy medical experts, prompting a broad and chaotic response nationwide. And the steak grew increasingly rancid. Leaders focused on social liberties and the importance of reopening the economy, dismissive of the health risks—sizzle. They insisted that children should return to schools—after all, the American education system is an important day care provider—so workers could return to work, despite the yet unclear health risks. More sizzle. The opportunities to mesmerize many with the sizzle amplified disharmony—at the leadership level, all the way to the individual level. The result included a noisy nation suffering a massive loss of life, financial destruction, eroding standing in the global community, and social and domestic discord that could take generations to correct. Because the approach neglected to focus first on the steak—the lives and well-being of American families—the United States was severely harmed on both the global and domestic stages.

Of course, the sizzle also required at least the illusion of action. Create a task force comprised of handpicked "experts" and administration leaders. Conduct frequent press conferences laced with hyperbole and self-promotion to emphasize that the pandemic is under control in an effort to show strength and control the message. Brand the initiative to develop a vaccine as "Operation Warp Speed." The controlled scurrying and classic branding were all sizzled. The steak did not exist. The task force proved largely unqualified and discordant due primarily to poor leadership. Messaging could not negate the realities of over half a million dead. More sizzle. Vaccines were produced in record time as the pharmaceutical companies raced to save the world. Steak. While the administration claimed credit, the only thing they did was buy the vaccines. Extraordinary leaders and scientists within the medical and pharmaceutical universes were exclusively responsible for developing, producing, and distributing the vaccine. *Steak.*

Beyond communicating with the citizens, the only material impacts the administration was accountable for included minimizing regulatory barriers to potential vaccine development and executing a comprehensive national distribution strategy. The administration effectively paved a path that accelerated vaccine development. Distribution proved to be all sizzle. The administration informed everyone that it was prepared to inoculate the country. By appointing a general to lead the initiative, the administration attempted to reassure Americans that the enemy would be defeated. However, no real strategy ever existed. *Sizzle.* After the scientific community delivered, all turned to "the plan." To the disappointment of many, the "plan" was really just an idea. *Sizzle.* This example of poor leadership was a costly illustration of noise rather than music. People died.

In contrast, the succeeding administration focused on the steak. They communicated a singular focus and emphasized it with urgency. They established meaningful goals, concentrating on "shots in arms" rather than how many vaccines were bought. While not entirely perfect in its execution, this focus on the steak, rather than the sizzle, likely saved lives and allowed commerce to return. Pundits argue that the different focuses were key to the outcome of the 2020 presidential election. The losers relied on the sizzle of their brand, relegating the basic needs of the voter—survival—as secondary. Conversely, the new administration focused predominantly on the basic needs and executed definitive plans to eliminate the existential threat, which mobilized record numbers of voters to the polls, determined to protect themselves and their communities from continued devastation and potential eradication. Steak beat sizzle. With this focus on each level of needs, the campaign earned enough trust to win a chance to lead the nation through existential adversity.

The DeLorean Motor Company was an American automobile manufacturer founded in 1975. In 1981, production began for DeLorean DMC-12. A car that was supposed to be safe, long-lasting, and sustainable. The vision excited prospective customers, investors, and the auto industry. Its iconic look with gull wing doors—the sizzle—hyped up the car to the masses, exciting the industry and generating considerable anticipation from customers and auto enthusiasts. The sizzle generated tremendous attention from stakeholders worldwide. The exclusivity of the "club" made owners feel like they were a part of a special family (belongingness). The innovative persona and perceived exclusivity were destined to turn heads and invite admiration from the masses (esteem). However, the steak suffered. The car did not meet the basic needs of any car owner. It failed to perform (basic needs). Maintenance was complicated and costly (safety/security). A cool-looking car is merely a piece of garage furniture if it does not drive. Because of the car's shoddy performance, DeLorean produced fewer than 9,000 cars and filed for bankruptcy. While still iconic, the futuristic DeLorean failed to deliver because leadership failed to pay proper attention to the steak.

Another example at a more microcosmic level is Pets.com. Launched in 1998, Pets.com was introduced as an online resource in a rapidly growing pet accessories and supplies segment. The vision recognized a trending desire for consumers to introduce convenience more substantially to their lives, and the retail segment was quick to answer the call. Significant investments were made in marketing and advertising, as well as impressive site design elements. The memorable sock puppet advertising campaign generated excited anticipation. All of the sizzle was encouraging to the investment community, as well, and more than $300 million in investment capital solidified confidence in the business plan. At first, it was a success. However, the critical absence of fundamental plug-and-play solutions for scalable shoppability (basic need), e-commerce management, and customer service (safety and security) quickly exposed a devastating lack of steak despite the very notable sizzle. Due to the brand's weak fundamentals, poor timing, and a myriad of other details, the three-hundred-million-dollar investment capital vanished along with the company.

The airline industry regularly faces challenges that affect customer satisfaction, employee satisfaction, and satisfaction among external constituents. The intense profitability challenges presented by a highly commoditized transportation landscape create a perpetually adverse environment. At the base, travelers seek a resource that will get them where they need to go reliably, affordably, safely, comfortably, and as quickly as possible. Selling this product for more than it costs to provide it is constantly a delicate dance, often stigmatizing the industry for poor service, poor punctuality records, and inequity in the customer's value equation ("Am I getting what I am paying for?"). General reputations of grumpy employees, poor or indifferent customer service, and diminished reliability constantly plague the industry and inhibit substantial efforts to enhance customer loyalty. Although significant successes in enhancing customer loyalty are driven by marketing programs, such as the various miles programs each airline offers, this sizzle does not do enough. Because a consistently good steak is not reliably expected, the sizzle of marketing campaigns and promotional activity are simply commoditized. While degrees of success vary from airline to airline, every airline competes on price. Every airline competes on miles programs. Every airline competes on access and punctuality. This commoditization made it increasingly important to find ways to satisfy the travelers' needs beyond the basic and safety levels. How the airline makes the traveler feel is increasingly important. At the core of the challenges to deliver a good steak are airline employees.

Southwest Airlines successfully identified a solution that strikes an efficient and adaptive balance between the needs levels. At the core of the solution was its employees. An industry veteran, the airline embarked on a human resources journey that transcended its original focus on employee satisfaction and talent acquisition and retention to enhance the customer experience. Through comprehensive consideration of each of the needs levels of the employees, the airline developed a team culture and managed to communicate its goals and vision to employees in a way that makes them a part of a unified team. Through credible empowerment actions, the airline emphasized policies and practices that give employees "permission" to go the extra mile to make customers happy, empowering them to do what they need to do to meet that vision. The resulting consumer-facing "Free to Move about the Cabin" campaign communicated a culture shift that differentiates Southwest from its competitors today. The sizzle of the campaign originated with an innovative human resources strategy, which supported the attitude and enhanced the customer experience. Although financial conditions continue to challenge the company's ability to support the culture, devotion to the culture has become part of the DNA, influencing most aspects of the operation.

Many examples of failures and successes in addressing the hierarchy of needs are comprehensively documented, and many more are constantly developing. The critical point is the importance of recognizing the need to provide all constituents, both internal and external, with a cultural focus on ensuring that the basic needs are always at the center of the efforts, creating greater potential for success by delivering steak before sizzle. Organizations that lose sight of the steak for the sizzle place themselves in unnecessary jeopardy. And this focus flows bidirectionally. Formulating plans to address adversity is often made easier by simply assessing how the organization is truly meeting the needs of each constituency.

> *Customer loyalty is eroding even though we have the best loyalty gimmicks in the industry.*
> *Employee turnover is unacceptably high. Customer service reviews are poor. Are the pizza parties and retention gimmicks just expenses that lead us to believe we are a good place to work?*
> *Economic conditions and industry trends are negatively affecting our performance. Our suppliers have become more rigid and less*

willing to share risk with us. Wall Street is not sympathetic, no matter how we package the story. Are we focusing our energies more on our needs and not enough on their needs in our conversations about surviving our challenges?

Despite impressive shows and presentations filled with rationalization, hope, and optimistic outlooks, our shareholders are shorting our stock. Why aren't they more loyal? Why aren't they more invested?

The logical first step toward addressing the matter is simply to ask, "Have we done everything possible to gain their trust? Is this relationship based more on *steak* than *sizzle*?" Obviously, this is far easier to say than do. However, to get there, the important thing is to remember to ask the question. Every time. By nature, the volume of the sizzle almost always threatens to overwhelm the content of the steak to the point that it is easily drowned out. That volume makes it even more important for someone to make sure the question is asked. High-performing leaders rarely have a problem making sure their organizations never lose sight of the steak. Dysfunctional leadership is more easily distracted. In these cases, the music is distorted, creating noise whose origin is difficult to identify. In these cases, an effective solution can be to go so far as to write down the needs of each constituency and then sincerely challenge how fully the needs are met on a consistent basis.

I believe we compensate our employees fairly. But do we really?

I am proud of our innovative programs that encourage creativity and inclusion. Does our leadership culture practically embrace these ideals? Is empowerment and respect just lip service?

We have chosen to emphasize our exclusive club to make our customers feel special. But do we really carry the products that they want and can afford?

Do we make it easy for our customers to buy from us?

Do our partners work with us to solve problems, or are we constantly on our own?

MUSIC. NOT NOISE

The results of this microscopic evaluation usually surprise leaders. Genuine self-assessments that are free of ego quickly pinpoint the exact issues that contribute to the erosion of the relationship with any constituency. Harmonious organizations do this effectively. Noisy organizations do not.

Empathetically acknowledging the needs that conceptually drive trust in relationships is essential for leaders to guide their organizations through adversity by prioritizing the steak before the sizzle. When sincerely and comprehensively applied, the result is often music, not noise. Despite how conceptually obvious this view may seem, the absence of this critical perspective is quite common, particularly among organizations that find themselves struggling with adversity. They sizzle out. Sizzle is noisy.

Chapter 10

Make Me Money or Save Me Money—Focus on Fundamental Purpose

To build on Dumas's premise that business is the simple matter of selling something for more than it costs to produce, the paramount responsibility of leaders is to ensure that all resources and activities focus, first, on a simple imperative: to either make money or save money for the organization. While seemingly oversimplified, focus on this principle is at the essential core of the success or failure of any organization, regardless of the million complexities that add dimension to decision-making. With every investment—whether in time, people, or various activities—comes the fiduciary obligation to deliver profit. High-performing organizations never lose sight of this obligation, while discordant organizations universally tend to blur the line. This blurring is often missed in the balance sheets because it becomes an organic trait enterprise-wide. As a result, discordant organizations contain a large number of nonproductive processes and a massive number of unemployed people on the payroll. These inconspicuously unproductive investments in time and resources significantly contribute to discord. Unproductive instruments in the orchestra create noise.

Recognizing the net-positive or net-negative elements of an organization is fairly simple. Operating budgets clearly quantify the cost or contribution of every component. These are easily identified as producing either a direct or indirect contribution to income or cost control and containment. However, particularly in mature organizations, blurring prompts leaders to create distinct types of contributions—simply classified as "hard" and "soft" contributions.

How does this function either make me money or save me money? How does this activity either make me money or save me money? How does this investment either make me money or save me money? We have thousands of dollars sitting around this table. Will this meeting contribute thousands of dollars in revenue or savings? Should this topic have been addressed via a series of emails or phone calls?

Hard contributions are straightforward. As an example, the sale of an item for more than it costs to produce contributes to hard gross profit. Effectively deployed technology solutions reduce and control costs, providing a more indirect contribution to profitability. Each of these is relatively easy to measure and control.

Soft contributions are more complex. Initiatives such as corporate social responsibility, for instance, are established business imperatives to solidify relationships with all levels of the constituency. However, the material value of CSR is rarely easy to quantify. It is when the answer to the simple profitability question becomes complicated that problems begin. While these, among many other brand-enhancing initiatives, indirectly enhance competitiveness, leaders often struggle to justify their existence, particularly in times of adversity.

Discordant organizations often contain functions, processes, and activities that produce complex answers to simple questions regarding making or saving money. These organizations often become increasingly burdened by investments that fit in the soft contribution category. In most cases, functions and activities designed to deliver soft benefits to an organization originate with beneficial intent. In many cases, distressed organizations allow lengthy lists of "untouchables," both by way of pet projects and personnel. In some cases, the benefits are ultimately measurable. In more cases, complex ROI analysis is applied to justify the choices. The question "How does this make or save me money?" becomes difficult to answer succinctly.

Do we have a long list of personnel whose value is difficult to quantify but cannot be eliminated?
Do we have a long list of pet projects whose value is difficult to quantify but cannot be eliminated?

Particularly among discordant organizations, "scope creep" threatens to erode bottom lines as disparate activities focusing on soft contribution become compounded over time. Often, entire departments are created to manage initiatives that are difficult to fiscally rationalize. This always hurts the ears of pitch-perfect leaders. A lack of diligent oversight allows scope creep to become embedded in the operation, like the woodwind section that is slightly off-key. As the orchestra compensates, the sour notes become less obvious. However, the result is noise rather than music.

Soft contributions come in a variety of sizes, shapes, and colors. From employee programs to corporate social responsibility to various luxuries justified as time-saving investments, the impact of these activities is often substantial and typically a significant contributor to organizational distress. The resources required to maintain the activities—people, money, and time—have immediate costs, while the benefits often require more patience than financial conditions can afford.

In any organization, soft contributions are viewed as accepted gray areas. Internal reviews of these activities are typically cumbersome, often resulting in inaction. Their existence is craftily validated. Productive organizations force themselves to view business operations with a more objective lens to effectively address the grayness, enabling them to quickly make appropriate choices. Discordant organizations get mired in the gray. Under adverse conditions, the importance of valuation exercise is often excruciating. Depending on the degree of distress, leaders in these organizations expend inordinate energies addressing simple measurements with emotional rationale. However, the soft contributors absolutely *must* be objectively assessed and prioritized. This assessment should *not* determine whether the investment should exist or not. Properly executed, this assessment should objectively *prioritize* the investments with other investments.

> *This social program differentiates us from our competitors and is also very meaningful to our employees. But is it worth the cost? Are we willing to keep the program in exchange for laying off ten productive employees?*
> *Our image requires us to present an impressive image. But does this costly office décor really influence our bottom line? Are our clients impressed? Or are they thinking that they are paying premium rates for our furniture?*
> *This group is really great at creating content. But would outsource the function at a fraction of the cost enable us to keep ten employees who more directly impact customers on a daily basis?*
> *We demand only the best. But does anyone objectively evaluate the value of the quality differences?*

The more complex the organization, the more difficult the task of maintaining fiscal efficiency discipline. Whether the investment exists to deliver hard or soft contributions, the original intent was to contribute to profitability. In either case, the leadership imperative demands diligent attention to the black-and-white questions. They must regularly assess whether any investment is either making money or saving money. No gray. Effective leaders tend to exercise the necessary focus and vision to drive efficiency. Distressed organizations commonly find themselves stuck in the gray muck, failing to simply and clearly identify the black-or-white contribution. The result is sour notes. The result is noise rather than music.

Chapter 11

Process Makes Perfect— Perfecting Fundamentals

A key difference between successful organizations and dysfunctional ones is the effective execution of fundamentals. These fundamentals include planning and process. Effective organizations identify where they want to go, plan a way to get there, and consistently institute processes that will most effectively and efficiently get them there. Importantly, harmonious organizations demand perfect fundamentals. Doing the small things perfectly ensures harmony. It is quite simple, no matter what kind of organization is involved. Great musicians, athletes, and leaders practice until they can no longer get it wrong. Poor performers stop practicing once they have gotten it right.

Planning is essential. Planning ensures that everyone knows where the organization wants to go and how it will get there. Warren Buffet is quoted as saying, "An idiot with a plan can beat a genius without a plan." He has a point. If you have not made it clear where you are going and how you will get there, you make noise. With every instrument playing from the same sheet music and every musician hearing the same desired sound, music is made.

While the value of formal plans seems obvious, the absence of a real plan is prevalent among struggling organizations.

How often is the organization obviously "winging it"?
When asked about strategic or tactical objectives, how often are the answers unclear, superficial, or even nonexistent?
How often is the answer inconsistent when asking multiple members of the organization at various levels?
When asked about specific and documented plans to ensure success, how often do leaders respond with "We are a simple company, not Amazon or Google. We don't need to complicate things with plans. We just get it done"?
How often do rank-in-file associates say they don't know what the plan is when asked?

The importance of the process is universally acknowledged. Every enterprise—regardless of sector, size, or age—eventually integrates processes and procedures designed to establish plans, standardize activities, create greater consistency, streamline productivity, enhance stakeholder experience, and optimize profitability. Whether through simple process mapping, technology integration, or a combination of various measures, the purest rationale for business process development and improvement initiatives focuses predominantly on bottom-line efficiency.

An effective process is one that produces the right results consistently. Jack Nicklaus once said, "Anyone can hit a golf ball a mile. The professional golfer is one who hits the ball a mile—every time!" In a perfect world, process efficiency easily translates into enhanced profitability. A diligent focus on bottom-line enhancement typically assures measurable success. Either the process investments directly improve profitability, or they do not. Focus on these, therefore, is critical to the effectiveness of any organization. An even more significant benefit of process discipline is its impact on brainpower—the efficient use of gray matter. Effective organizations maintain a fine balance between activities that enhance productivity through operational process improvement and maintenance and creative thinking. By making fundamental tasks second nature, they enable and inspire the kind of creative thinking and problem-solving that dramatically improves performance.

Our processes are so well-tuned that the company could practically run itself.
Our processes are world-class, and we follow them religiously.
Is it easy for a new employee to follow the bouncing ball?
We have high levels of employee loyalty, but when we bring in talented new people, they often get frustrated and leave.
Why are we working so hard to do something so simple?
Why are we constantly missing launch deadlines?
Why does something so simple as processing a payment seem so difficult?
Why is our product so many shades of the same color? We only have one shade!

Some of the greatest football coaches in history have provided numerous examples of the importance of perfected fundamentals. Every good football coach always devotes a portion of practice time to game fundamentals before any energy is devoted to game strategy. Win or lose, every good football coach gets the team back to the practice field to focus first on fundamentals. The minute mechanics are drilled into the players' minds until they consistently become second nature. Successful coaches drill fundamental activities into muscle memory. Then, and only then, do successful coaches allow their players to spend any energy on playing the game. Consequently, their teams tend to miss fewer blocks, commit fewer penalties, and lose fewer games.

After a disappointing loss or string of losses, the first thing most great coaches do is reaffirm a tireless emphasis on fundamentals. These leaders refocus their teams on the basics of the game. Block. Tackle. Mental discipline. They refuse to allow their teams to "play the game" despite the unrest this tactic causes among players who are programmed to compete. Eventually, the players' discomfort with the drudgery subsides, and fundamental excellence returns. Then the players are allowed to compete.

This lesson applies to any organization. A notable distinction between exceptional organizations and dysfunctional organizations is the discipline with which they address fundamentals at every level.

Dysfunctional organizations practice fundamentals until they "get it right," while exceptional organizations practice fundamentals until they can no longer get it wrong. The most meaningful difference between the two approaches is the sustained outcome—especially regarding productivity and efficiency. By eliminating or minimizing fundamental errors, exceptional organizations create "muscle memory" that creates consistent performance and enables functional focus on solutions, efficiency, and creativity. Conversely, organizations that find themselves mired in a constant struggle to "get it right" expend costly energy on processes rather than optimal outcomes.

Distressed organizations typically exhibit process breakdowns that impede efficiency. More organizations than one might imagine lacking any formal process in most areas, if any at all. The result is a noisy performance that drowns out the music. Harmonious organizations effectively recognize often obvious symptoms of process failure or disruption, while distressed organizations do not. Some of these symptoms include the following:

- Task duplication
- Misaligned task allocation ("I got it, you got it, nobody's got it.")
- Ineffective task transition
- Process complexity (too many steps, complicating what should be simple)
- Process inconsistency (multiple unique tweaks to established procedures)
- Cycle time delays
- Inconsistent quality (product, communication, service, support)
- Breakdowns in simple processes (especially when disruptive factors are introduced)

Whether a professional football team, a Fortune 500 corporation, a national government, or a family unit, the value of this principle applies. Most organizations practice fundamentals until they finally get it right. The most successful organizations are those that practice fundamentals until they can no longer get it wrong. The difference becomes tangibly noticeable when something disrupts operational harmony.

Processes often take on a perpetual life of their own. They evolve from being a means to an end to becoming the ends within themselves. They easily become a part of the organizational DNA that requires individual investment and attention. By nature, they are adopted because their routine nature makes them comforting. Unchecked, this evolution can easily become a hindrance, rather than an impetus, to optimal productivity. They become the noise that disrupts harmony. And because they tend to consume increasing brainpower and forced rigidity, they inhibit critical organizational creativity. An effective process produces the right results consistently. Particularly for distressed organizations, process breakdowns are often a cause of adversity. Notably, process breakdowns are almost *always* a symptom. Leaders of these organizations neglect some of the key indicators and rarely have the time and resources to hear the noise. By asking some simple questions, identifying process opportunities can be easy. Central to self-examination is a request for process documents for various functions. As Edward Demings wrote, "If you can't describe what you are doing as a process, you don't know what you are doing." More often than not, discordant organizations either do not have these documents or the documents are unnecessarily complex. As Einstein said, "If you can't explain what you are doing simply, you don't understand it well enough." Whether no process documentation exists or existing documentation is too complicated, either is an indicator of dysfunction that causes or contributes to large problems.

McDonald's became a classic example of a multilayered and overly complex process that led to an executional dysfunction. The core competence of the fast-food giant was the standardized creation, production, and delivery of burgers, fries, and beverages. To maximize profits and ensure consistent quality standards in the rapidly growing fast-food industry, the company developed a comprehensive 750-page operations manual that governed processes worldwide. However, growing competitive challenges from Burger King and Taco

Bell exposed opportunities associated with shifting consumer taste profiles. These profiles were not considered in what would become a 750-page doorstop in McDonald's offices around the globe. The myopic process-driven culture at McDonald's made nimble adjustments to these market shifts cumbersome, resulting in slow process reengineering and ineffective product launches. Their recognition of the need for process standardization was well-grounded. Their process overcomplication made them less able to respond to sudden consumer and competitive shifts, costing them growth opportunities and share erosion. Through time, astute leadership learned that the manual was hardly ever used. They realized that the focus of its development was on creating a comprehensive manual rather than a simple road map that ensured executional consistency worldwide. They quickly simplified the process, which resulted in a brief guide to executional excellence.

Many of the daily operations of any organization involve tactical performance. Most of the daily expectations of effective leaders focus on creativity. To find harmony, leaders must frequently review all areas of the organization to ensure that fundamentals are consistently maintained and creative thinking is encouraged. While the tangible components of operational process creation and improvement are relatively easy to recognize, the equally valuable benefit is the liberation of creative thinking and creative problem-solving. Because they are so relatively easy to understand, the tangibles typically receive exclusive attention. The plethora of process improvement experts provides a wealth of value to any organization, regardless of current business conditions. Under adverse conditions, the focus on tangible process optimization is invaluable and necessarily receives prompt attention. Exceptional leaders return to fundamentals when the organization is underperforming.

While this focus on fundamentals is critical, perhaps even more critical is the optimization of time to apply creative thinking and problem-solving. Under adverse conditions, leaders are too easily consumed by tactical activities, thus disallowing them the time or focus necessary to address creative solutions to performance challenges.

PROCESS MAKES PERFECT

In organizations with process voids, leaders spend all their time and energy on blocking and tackling rather than analysis and strategy development execution. It is natural. Whether due to "squeaky wheel syndrome" or natural reversion to easier, more familiar tasks, people at all levels address the obvious and easy. The black-and-white issues monopolize their attention. The gray matter becomes the victim.

Are our leaders thinking and behaving too much like followers? Are our conversations too focused on how the watch is made rather than what time it is?

Not every activity requires sophisticated process mapping, but very few do not. By diligently attending to continuous process improvement and capitalizing on liberated time that enables creative thinking and problem-solving, effective leaders produce a harmonious performance. Because rote functions divert their time and energy, tone-deaf leaders labor to create a sound, forsaking the desired musicality.

Chapter 12

You Eat What You Kill—Hunt Wisely. Defend Diligently. Consume Efficiently.

Globally, choice is greater for consumers than at any time in the history of commerce. Driven largely by innovation and opportunity, the availability of options, as well as access to these perennially expanding options, creates a dynamic competitive landscape for leaders responsible for capturing and protecting share. As the hunting grounds shrink, hungry competitors proliferate and aggressively invade territories.

This existential challenge illuminates the importance of intelligent, adaptive strategies that ensure that hunting grounds are realistically identified and protected, prey is abundant and robust enough to provide more energy to the predator than is required to survive, and the hunter—whether solitary or social—operates in an efficient and unified manner. Those who do it well survive. Those who do not, perish.

Successful businesses clearly and consistently develop and execute competitive strategies that focus on identifying and quantifying efficient market opportunities, mitigating competitor impact, demanding efficient and adaptive execution, and inspiring a Killer Instinct. They create and execute clear and consistent offensive and defensive strategies designed to deliver returns greater than the cost. They do this regardless of their industry position. They integrate this thinking into all strategic considerations without exception. Dysfunctional organizations often do not. The results are sales and customer loss, significant profit erosion, and, ultimately, death by starvation.

That is a comprehensive and valid plan, but how will our competition respond? What is our plan for that?

The foundation of an effective and comprehensive competitive strategy is the existence of one, a real one. These strategies address three unique competitive tiers:

- Organic
- Incremental
- Exponential

Organic competitive strategies address plans to grow and protect existing businesses without any additional resource expenditure or allocation. Maintain and protect.

Incremental competitive strategies address plans to generate additive growth to the *existing* portfolio, whether at the portfolio or business unit. This plan leverages *existing* competencies and capabilities and requires limited, if any, resource investment. This strategic tier can include expansion of existing customer segments, product and service offerings, and geographic expansion.

Internal incremental growth is similarly additive and includes controlled expansion of resources and processes determined necessary to ensure revenue growth or cost containment through process improvement.

Exponential competitive strategies address additive growth opportunities that leverage core competencies and capabilities but are not currently a component of the portfolio. Exponential growth is applied at the universal (portfolio) level as well as the individual level (SBU, products, services, markets, infrastructure, systems, and processes). Exponential growth often, but not necessarily, requires resource investments associated with expansion.

Within each tier, a sound competitive strategy addresses two simple components—offense and defense. These components ensure profitable customer acquisition and retention while protecting the organization from competitor incursion. They concentrate on capturing prey while protecting the hunting grounds.

The offensive component of a competitive strategy requires focus. As it is often said, "A fox who chases two rabbits will catch neither." Effective strategies constantly pursue innovative methods to identify, capture, and defend profitable revenue opportunities but maintain a discipline that disallows distraction.

Diversification is a common example of how organizations can lose focus. Developed with good intentions, many distressed organizations invest in plans to enhance their markets through consumer or geographic expansion, core competence extension, or innovation. In some cases, this works. Effective leaders adopt innovative expansion strategies that are disciplined and maintain focus on the core DNA of the organization. They refuse to try to become someone they are not. Tone-deaf leaders do not. Lack of disciplined focus seduces these leaders into exciting endeavors that distract attention, divert valuable and limited resources, and initiate powerful profit erosion.

This does not mean an organization should never consider opportunities to diversify. Many successful organizations today are an evolved version of what they began as. However, the execution of these diversification strategies involved substantial risk assessment, unidimensional impact, and success measurement. Effective leaders who allow these types of risks diligently monitor and measure their results. These leaders embrace fidelity to the necessity of focus. They passionately adopt the "fail fast, fail cheap" mindset, allowing and inspiring innovative thinking, but require an exit plan as part of the strategy to ensure cost-efficient escape. They take calculated risks. And if the spoils cost more than the effort, they quickly call off the chase.

Among dysfunctional organizations, this focus is often obscured by myopic agendas, optimistic expectations, and a lack of discipline. Dysfunctional organizations execute unique diversification initiatives without controls. Additionally, these leaders fail to acknowledge the importance of "fail fast, fail cheap" as their myopic desire for success prompts them to increase their investment long after the initiative demonstrates damaging implications. Finally, the fear of bailing out too soon promotes unproductive determination to continue the initiative despite its impact on the overall organization. Ultimately, they throw good money after bad and fail to compete.

> *This initiative is not performing as we anticipated. We need to pour more resources into it, even though that means we will have to divert those resources from the core business.*
> *I still believe this is the right way to go, even though the numbers say otherwise. I think it's too soon to give up.*
> *We've invested so much time and resources into this; we must continue. In for a penny, in for a pound.*
> *I've staked my reputation on this initiative. It must not fail. Failure will cost me my job and my reputation.*

Pigs get fat. Hogs get slaughtered. Passion for innovation and diversification encourages leaders to seek incremental or alternative food sources. Some of those sources simply feed the caloric needs of the organization, while many expand it. Focus, therefore, ensures a healthy balance. Unfocused efforts can easily overshadow disciplined growth strategies, luring tone-deaf leaders into unproductive rabbit holes. Most expansion ideas are born from good intentions. Some produce. Most do not. Disciplined focus ensures that organizations maintain focus and are prepared to exit a strategy when necessary. Abandoning a plan that is not working is not a failure. Blindly adhering to a failing plan is. Effective leaders recognize this. Tone-deaf leaders do not.

Another imperative that is often overlooked is efficiency. Expending one thousand calories to capture prey that only provides one hundred calories starves an organization. Occasionally, tactics such as "loss leader" programs serve the greater mission. However, particularly in highly commoditized industries, this inefficiency induces a slow starvation that only becomes noticeable once the organization appears frail and fragile.

> *Are we still hungry after the hunt?*
> *Are we missing opportunities because we are casting nets rather than dropping a line in the water?*

Are we constantly trying to find creative ways to stretch the margin on sales with already slim margins?
Are our margins consistently low compared to our industry? Compared to economic indicators?

Passion to innovate and necessity-driven market expansion excite people in any organization. The combination of competitive necessity and the allure of novelty promotes growth strategies. The most significant and measurable area impacted is net profit. Effective growth strategies demand a disciplined focus on profit balance in their tactics. Tone-deaf strategies fail. They expend more energy to catch the prey than they get after consuming the prey.

More than ever, a constantly adaptive mentality is an existential imperative for any organization. Failure to adapt is a core trait of almost every distressed organization. To consistently feed the organization with new product revenue, new markets, and new customers, a nimble adaptive mentality is necessary. Nimbly adapting to the way people consume products and information is essential. Adaptive thinking and technology are the core enablers. Effective leaders adapt quickly. Tone-deaf leaders do not.

Has our sales strategy fallen behind technology and consumer trends? Why is our sales and marketing budget still predominantly allocated to paper communication when everyone is staring at their phones today?
Are we communicating with our customers and prospects the way that they prefer rather than what is most convenient for us?
Are we still selling buggy whips while everyone is driving cars?
Does our advertising reflect our market today? Does it look dated? Does it sound dated? Is the messaging dated? Are we just talking to ourselves?

Perhaps the most intangible trait of any organization is a Killer Instinct. It is necessary. It is that gut drive and determination to win that is impossible to measure. Killer Instinct is innate in any successful organization and is especially evident in effective sales organizations. The thrill of the hunt is far greater than the feast afterward. Killer Instinct must be controlled, however, to ensure that the rewards outweigh the risks. If unchecked, calculated risks become the costly victims. The sales executive who is excited by the prospect of the kill but neglects consideration for what it will cost to make the kill can be destructive. Effective leaders recognize this. Tone-deaf leaders do not.

Adversity presents a significant opportunity to evaluate this quality in any organization. Especially when addressing adverse conditions, attitudes expose those who have the instinct and those who do not. To recognize its existence, effective leaders pay attention to attitudinal and behavioral cues that simply are not exposed in conventional business metrics. Those who possess Killer Instincts are energized by adversity and immediately turn their attention to assertive actions to correct negative trends through a focus on revenue generation and optimization.

> *Is our sales approach predominantly passive?*
> *Do our sales programs reflect an assumption that they will come to us just because we are here? Do we think people will give us money just because?*
> *Does our historic prominence lull our sales activities into complacency?*
> *When was the last time we discussed an innovative way of acquiring new customers or retaining existing customers?*
> *Is our sales organization too comfortable?*
> *Why is our sales department so quiet? Shouldn't the energy level be higher?*
> *When discussing negative revenue trends, how many in our company sit helplessly on the sideline? How many immediately turn their attention to solving the sales challenge? How many simply claim "It's not my fault"?*

On the defensive spectrum of competitive strategy, the requirements are the same. Focus, efficiency, nimbleness, and Killer Instinct are necessary to successfully defend the established hunting territory.

Any organization that believes the competition is not working on ways to steal their prey is foolish. Effective leaders always consider their individual and collective competitors in competitive strategies, dedicating substantial attention to plans to protect their existing territory while identifying methods to safely capture competitor territories. The most effective leaders are those who anticipate competitor strategies and responses and plan accordingly. For example, when developing a plan to expand into a new geographic market, the most effective leaders plan for the incumbent competitors to react. They refuse to assume that the competitors are going to passively allow them to take their business. Thus, their plans include tactics to offset anticipated competitor response. Effective leaders often integrate comprehensive historical insights into their planning to efficiently predict likely competitor responses.

> *What are the common responses each of our key competitors have when anyone launches a new product that competes with theirs?*
> *What are the common responses of each of our relevant competitors when they learn someone is planning to open a new location in their markets?*
> *Internally, who is responsible for maintaining a dynamic competitor activity database? How is that database used?*

A common mistake tone-deaf leaders make is improperly identifying their true competition. Too often, these leaders limit their competitor assessments to those who are most like them. Lions who defend their territory against other big cats expose themselves to encroachment by hyenas and wild dogs, as well as vultures patiently waiting for the lion to expend the calories for the kill before consuming the calories for themselves. Organizations that fail to consider every entity trying to capture the same consumer frequently fall victim to surprisingly unexpected customer erosion.

This myopic perspective is often evident in the highly commoditized fast-moving consumer goods (FMCG) sector, where leading manufacturers and retail partners tend to focus on like organizations. Meanwhile, after-market, gray market, and "knockoff" manufacturers and retail outlets stealthily erode formerly sound customer bases with the appeal of lower prices and greater convenience. Any conventional supermarket chain serves as a tangible example. Once the sole source of groceries and personal products, these leaders denied the obvious increase in channel blurring, ignoring the appeal of companies like Walmart and Costco. Over time, the nimbler leaders acknowledged the changing channel landscape and adjusted accordingly. The less nimble leaders failed.

Again, a Killer Instinct is perhaps the most critical trait in defensive competitive strategies. This instinct is pervasive at all levels in successful organizations. Their strategic and tactical approaches are assertive rather than passive. They bring the fight to the competition rather than waiting. Passive defense is the most revealing quality of tone-deaf leaders.

> *What is our concerted strategy to eliminate our competition?*
> *How often do we discuss competitor strategies?*
> *What is our strategy when a competitor reveals intentions to move into our market?*
> *Do our strategic plans anticipate a competitor response?*

Passive defense is easy to identify in failing retail companies and is alarmingly more common than one would imagine. When asked about their plans to combat new competitor store openings, distressed organizations can offer little. Often, the response is to simply adjust budgets based on sometimes historical data quantifying average impact. They allow the competitor to invade their territory and fail to mount a serious defense.

> *They usually hit us for about 25 percent, so we just adjust our budgets to reflect a 25 percent sales decline.*

Successful retailers refuse to accept this assumption. Effective leaders inspire their organizations to analyze competitor tactics in an effort to identify key areas of strength and weakness—both internal and competitor. They proactively create competitor strategies that ensure a thorough understanding of tactics they can expect as competitors launch growth plans encroaching on their territory.

Especially in terms of geographic expansion, competitors in the retail space are often predictable. They broadcast prospective target geographies and tend to execute largely prescriptive launch strategies. Effective retailers know when permit applications are submitted and have prepared competitor response plans ready to implement. These plans are multidimensional, involving all areas of operation, including human resources, marketing, merchandising, pricing, and promotion. Effective retailers know that a successful fresh grocer will target top fresh department employees with enticements to join them and enhance employee engagement across the target store with a particular focus on the fresh departments. Effective retailers acknowledge internal vulnerabilities that competitors will likely attack and work diligently to eliminate them. Effective retailers know what the competitor's promotional calendar will include and execute merchandising, pricing, and promotion plans designed to weaken the potential of the loss leaders by compelling the market to buy them prior to the new store opening—removing the demand.

Simply eliminating potential competition is another effective tactic. Most effective retailers strategically invest in vacant properties targeted by competitors to prevent the competitors from acquiring them. They acknowledge that it is unrealistic to assume any plans will remove the greater threat but endeavor to mitigate the anticipated impact as much as possible at local levels. Killer Instinct drives them to plan for attack and swiftly act when competitors begin execution. Tone-deaf retailers just adjust their budgets down and hope for the best.

And then there is the case of Black & Decker. Founded in 1910, the company prospered for decades, establishing itself as a global leader in power tools and accessories. However, the competitive landscape became increasingly aggressive, and the once prominent brand was severely tarnished. Leadership pointed out that the B&D image was more like FP (Fisher-Price). In a growing DIY market, this was not good.

In the early 1990s, under the leadership of Nolan Archibald, the company developed and executed a remarkable plan. Archibald and his team realized that a competitive acquisition from nearly thirty years earlier could be an ideal vehicle to revive his brand with the growing "weekend warrior" market, as well as his stakeholders. Sitting on the dusty shelves of a remote warehouse were several items that were created by potential competitors to Black & Decker but now belonged to the company. One of these items was a power drill still encased in a heavy gray metal casing. However, Archibald instructed his teams to create a strategy around this acquired asset. What was once an acquisition to remove a potential threat was about to become a tool of revitalization.

The team addressed the challenge multidimensionally, starting with a comprehensive understanding of the new power tool consumer. Their profile revealed that the new weekend warriors required a professional level but affordable performance. Importantly, they wanted to feel like they were on a construction site. One of the common characteristics of construction sites at the time was the color yellow, so the product revision included high-performance cordless technology in a yellow casing. Next, the team partnered with select retailers to execute marketing programs that included mobile on-site product demonstrations in their parking lots. These mobile units reflected a construction site atmosphere, piquing the interest of the target audience.

Finally, Black & Decker relaunched DeWalt. What once collected dust in a dark, remote Maryland warehouse became the catalyst of competitive growth for a struggling company. The successful and sustained launch revived the portfolio's position in the industry, as well as among stakeholders. Additionally, the launch was so successful that it provided enough profits to mitigate a nearly disastrous debt obligation obtained as a result of a highly leveraged Emhart acquisition.

As Darwin asserted, the survival of the fittest favors those who adapt. Those who fail, perish. Capturing and protecting valuable territory requires focus, efficiency, and a Killer Instinct. Nobody is going to kill it for you. Nobody is going to hand-feed you. Your competitors are not going to meekly concede territory. You either hunt successfully, become the prey, or starve to death.

Chapter 13

Control the Message, or It Will Control You—the Communication Imperative

Communication has been one of the foundational pillars of society at every level. Whether through words, gestures, cave drawings, fanned tail feathers, or billions of other communicative cues, sharing information is crucial to societal survival. Adversity introduces uncomfortable change. Change raises questions. Adversity-induced change exponentially amplifies questions.

When questions are not satisfactorily answered, people inevitably fill those voids with often inaccurate or incomplete answers. Regardless of conditions, the importance of a comprehensive communication strategy is frequently underrated or overlooked, especially during challenging times. Regardless of the complexity of the challenge or the organization, the simple tenet is to *control the message, or the message will control you.*

By nature, people need answers to help them understand and cope with changes that may affect their lives. In the case of distressed organizations, these questions become intensified by fear, anxiety, and curiosity. From the line to management, customers to influencers, and partners to bankers, all stakeholders have a series of questions that must be answered. These questions range from existential to tactical practicalities. Like missing notes to a piece of music, these questions rarely go unanswered. In many cases, the answers are incomplete or inconsistent. In more cases, the answers are created from discordant information and any of a number of disparate sources. Whatever information is available is typically translated through personal lenses that rarely match reality. The noise created makes corrective efforts difficult.

Depending on the complexity of the challenges, as well as the universe of individuals and interests affected, the questions that require answers are extensive, diverse, and complicated. However, they tend to be easy to categorize. The audiences, too, can be complex and diverse. These audiences include the following:

- Employees
- Stakeholders
- Partners
- Industry
- Media

Both the questions and the audiences can contribute to a practical structure for a communication hierarchy that can be easily applied to a comprehensive communication strategy that is unique to the specific issues.

Exceptional leaders compose and direct performance from all chairs within the organization. They provide each employee, at every level, with the tools, information, and inspiration to succeed. While it is unrealistic to expect that every employee will agree with the decisions of management, it is realistic to expect that every employee will execute the directives in a concerted manner that produces results as long as the goals are clear and leadership is credible. As long as the tools, information, and inspiration are responsibly thought out and obviously available, success is more possible. The communication challenge management faces revolves around what questions employees have and what answers should be provided. The diversity of questions, both expected and unexpected, usually fits into an easily applied hierarchy.

At the base of the hierarchy are existential questions. Employees are people. They work to provide the best quality of life possible for themselves and their loved ones. The acknowledgment of organizational challenges, therefore, sparks existential questions that must be addressed in a believable, respectful, and consistent manner. Simply put, plain and complete answers are critical. The truth is essential. No matter how committed they are to the organization, employees are ultimately loyal to themselves first. To expect otherwise is foolish and irresponsible. The line between "culture" and "cult" is a fine one. Exceptional leaders always acknowledge and are prepared to address the personal concerns, whether spoken or unspoken, these stakeholders naturally feel. Astute anticipates these concerns. Tone-deaf leaders do not.

Am I going to lose my job?
Will my duties and responsibilities change?
Will my income be negatively affected?
Will my benefits be negatively affected?

The most predominant and most difficult question for internal stakeholders processing signals of adversity concerns personal security. The slightest hint of difficulty sparks conjecture and rumors of layoffs and job loss. Always. Without exception. This absolute can easily consume the workforce, creating noisy performance influenced by the distraction of the unknown. The greatest challenge for leaders is determining how to answer this relentless question. They are unsure if reductions in force will be appropriate solutions. They are unsure when reductions in force might occur. They are concerned that any announcements of potential reductions will initiate an exodus. Because of their uncertainty, most leaders choose to answer this question sparingly, if at all. If this most existential question *is* addressed, many leaders wait too long to share as little as possible. In most instances, this tactic creates greater confusion, distraction, and the loss of valuable talent.

One of the more effective tactics to prevent self-inflicted difficulties is to address the elephant in the room with honesty, sincerity, and openness. Speak factually. Speak sincerely. Speak openly.

Ultimately, actions are all that matters. However, the words at this critical juncture help to acknowledge the importance of and include the entire workforce in addressing the challenges. In the case of a distressed health care company composed of highly skilled, highly educated, and highly motivated professionals, measured transparency was necessary to maintain harmony and prevent exodus.

> *We realize that recent developments have made you concerned about your jobs. Rest assured that we are aggressively taking steps to make sure that your futures here are secure. We don't have all the answers, but we promise to work diligently to find the right solutions to protect everyone's future. Of course, your top question is "Will I lose my job?" Of course, you are concerned about that. We wish we could answer that question right now, but we cannot. What we will promise are the following:*
>
> 1. *If layoffs are necessary, we will have exhausted all other options carefully and responsibly.*
> 2. *If layoffs are necessary, they will occur in one fell swoop rather than piecemeal so that those remaining will not be looking over their shoulders for the next wave.*
> 3. *Finally, if layoffs are necessary, we will conduct the process with dignity. We will do everything in our power to treat those affected respectfully and compassionately.*

The approach, which is the cornerstone of several subsequent communication strategies, accomplished the objective. Talent rallied to collectively solve the problems that were beyond their control. They made music. They saved their company. A few years later, they enjoyed a successful and individually lucrative merger with a powerful national healthcare organization.

This level of transparency can be difficult and uncomfortable. Many leaders instinctively dismiss it as too complicated and revealing. However, the proactive approach respects the people, controls the message, and includes them in the difficult tasks that lie ahead. As long as the message is credible and consistent, the approach works.

The next tier of the hierarchy continues to be translated through a personal lens, but more about how their daily routines are affected. A dedicated workforce requires mission clarity to perform effectively.

They need to know what is expected of them at a functional level to deliver music. Of course, there are countless other variables that contribute to effective performance. However, the basics of how they spend their days must always be reasonably clear. Typically, among many things, they want to know the following:

Are my duties going to change?
Will my hours be affected?
Will my team structure change?
Will I be reporting to someone new?

The final tier of the hierarchy tends to be more global. Once the uniquely personal questions are clearly addressed, attention then turns to broader issues that generally center on personal relationships with the organization and others outside their intimate worlds.

How will my friends and colleagues be affected?
How will my customers be affected?
How will my business partners be affected?
How is this going to affect our Global Mission?

External audiences play an important role. Business partners, suppliers, investors, bankers, media, and customers require information unique to themselves to ensure the successful implementation of growth strategies. Like employees, each of these groups requires answers to questions based on a simple hierarchy, beginning with the existential, then practical/tactical, and then global.

External stakeholders are rarely involved in operational matters and are intimately interested in the bottom-line performance. Investors, board members, lenders, and regulatory agencies all have unique questions that must be answered. Their questions are driven by financial risk, initially at the personal level.

Is my capital at risk?
How will this affect my personal standing?
What will my bosses think?

Secondarily, a broader view drives broader questions.
How will my overall portfolio be affected?
Finally, more global questions arise.
What does this mean to the industry?
How will this affect my organization's global portfolio?

Partners also require answers that impact their decisions. They are predominantly suppliers involved in the production of products or services provided by the affected organizations or partners involved in product distribution, support, or a variety of other services. While the nature of what these organizations do may be peripheral, answers to their unique questions are important. For example, if a carmaker decides to close a plant, component suppliers will lose projected revenue, people will lose jobs, the local tax base will be affected, and more. With partners, the information needs hierarchy remains the same, beginning with personal/existential concerns, followed by broader issues, and then by more global interests.

Will I lose my job?
How will this affect my lifestyle?
How will this affect my organization?
With whom will I partner on a day-to-day basis?
What will this do to the industry landscape?
How will this affect our global strategy?

Lastly, the evolving media universe requires answers to their own unique set of questions. This is a universe that has become exponentially complex as information consumption grows more rapidly and diversely with the evolution of digital media. Additionally, this audience is strongly driven by factors unique to its discipline. The competitive focus on timeliness, along with a greater focus on uncovering newsworthy details underlying relevant conditions, makes this audience especially important when considering a communication strategy. They are skeptics, and they seek the sensational. It is about the story, not the situation. While the information needs of this audience are different from those of other audiences, the hierarchy is the same. From personal to global, members of this audience require answers. Depending on circumstances unique to the organization, matters of timeliness and consistency are most important.

At the personal level, members of this audience are similar to others but slightly unique.

> *Can I scoop my competition?*
> *Is there a story within this story that will win me recognition from my boss, peers, and industry?*
> *How can this story enhance the position and credibility of my organization?*

In all cases, the diverse audiences interested in developments affecting the organization require answers. Truth, timeliness, reliability, and consistency are essential. Without these answers, each will translate information through their unique lenses and fill in the blanks. This translation creates noise. Distracting, frustrating, exhausting, relentless noise.

Often, dysfunctional organizations fail to recognize the importance of a coordinated and disciplined communication strategy when taking action to correct declining performance. Why is a communication strategy, complete with process and policy, often overlooked when addressing corrective measures? The reasons vary and are commonly influenced by a multitude of factors involving resources, minimization, and culture.

> *It's just talking. We know how to do that.*
> *We should refrain from saying anything until there is something to say.*
> *We already have a communication policy/procedure and trust those responsible for disseminating the messages to do their jobs effectively. Our employees know that we are doing everything expected to protect the organization. Our results will answer every question they have.*

Under normal circumstances, existing communication policies and procedures are usually satisfactory. However, challenge prompts change. Change prompts questions. Questions require answers. Unique change requires unique answers.

One of the characteristics of organizations experiencing significant challenges relates to a *paternalistic* culture. A paternalistic culture is not necessarily good or bad. However, a paternalistic management culture often impedes communication. The admission of poor performance is not easy. Paternalistic cultures contain the additional layer of complexity associated with transparency. In each case, these emotionally driven conditions prevent the development of a comprehensive communication strategy.

One company that exuded paternalism is a family-owned regional firm that has occupied a prominent position for generations. Their culture emphasizes family, and employee loyalty has been extraordinary. Historical ownership created and fostered an ongoing culture of trust and dependence that proved successful and drove prominence in the industry. Competition and failure to evolve with the industry and consumers quickly initiated performance declines that threatened the firm's future. After years of success and good news, the owners faced unfamiliar challenges. Among these challenges was growing demands for information from all audiences. Creditors, labor unions, suppliers, and employees were curious about the causes and strategies prompted by unusual declines. Answers were required. An ingrained paternalistic culture made communication difficult. Everyone associated with the organization found comfort in the family's track record of effectively handling challenges, but the new challenges were different. Paternalistic communication attitudes would not suffice. Transparency was required. Creditors refused to accept "We're taking care of it" as an answer. Suppliers and long-standing labor unions refused to accept superficial or nonexistent responses to existential questions. Employees who were sheltered from bad news lost confidence in the trusted owners as they suffered financially and operationally. "Daddy is taking care of things" no longer worked. However, paternalistic cultures are difficult to correct, especially in a company that was on its third generation of the same ownership family. It was like many nuclear families.

Parents tend to avoid discussing bad things with their children. They want to protect their children. They believe they are responsible for fixing problems. They find it difficult to expose their personal failures to their children. They find transparency too uncomfortable.

This paternalistic company was exactly like that. The third generation of owners struggled to acknowledge the value of strategic transparency. Only after accepting the fact that strategic transparency was appreciated by both internal and external audiences did the owners accept a communication strategy that fostered inclusion rather than paternalism. The result was revitalized commitment from both internal and external stakeholders to contribute to solving the problems. That company still exists.

Finally, communication paralysis plays a significant role in the development of a comprehensive communication strategy. In many cases, leaders struggle to determine how much information to share and with whom it should be shared. This paralysis typically results in silence. After all, it is safer to say little or nothing rather than share too much.

How much is too much?
To whom should I communicate, and to what degree of specificity?
The media hates us. We should just avoid talking to them because they'll just twist everything to paint us negatively.

The difficulties exacerbated by ineffective communication strategies tailored specifically to the challenges an organization is facing are often undetected until it is too late. This unpredictability, along with the typically operational and cultural barriers, make it especially important for organizations to proactively include a communication component in their course correction strategies. Depending on the significance of the issue and organizational complexities (e.g., size, industry, stakeholder composition, etc.), a well-composed strategy can make the difference between success and failure.

So what works? Of course, unique situations require unique solutions. Structurally, a commonly effective approach is to establish a strategy that does the following:

- Categorizes audiences.
- Categorizes information levels.
- Identifies authorized spokespersons.
- Anticipates key questions (FAQs).
- Creates *consistent* messages.
- Creates communication frequency guidelines (e.g., memoranda, town halls, conference calls, etc.) to most effectively manage audience expectations.

This approach involves three components:

1. A structural chart identifying and defining both the type of information requests anticipated and the functional levels and individuals authorized to respond to the requests.
2. A variation of a responsibilities and accountabilities (RASCI) chart that diagrams and maps the audiences, information category, and how requests are channeled to ensure the appropriate individuals respond to the question.
3. A comprehensive list of frequently asked questions accompanied by proactively developed answers to ensure timely and consistent responses.

The structural chart categorizes types of information or questions based on internally determined degrees of sensitivity and potential implications to the organization. This structure makes it clear who is authorized to answer what kind of question and when the question should be referred to someone else in the organization. Properly employed, this structure prevents the possibility of misinformation and inconsistent messaging. An employee who is a union member, for instance, cannot share inaccurate information directly with union leadership and members, thus eliminating the potential for virality that exacerbates the situation.

Generally, the types of questions received can be categorized into three levels:

> *Level one—basic:* insignificant importance, nominal risk, superficial, involves information generally already existing in the public domain
>
> *Level two—moderate:* escalated inquiry; moderate significance; more detailed; requires information most appropriately provided by specialists, such as finance, R&D, etc.; requests forward-thinking/strategy information; potentially involves proprietary, confidential information; implications could include legal, regulatory, or financial exposure
>
> *Level three—sensitive:* includes questions pertaining to highly sensitive information; proprietary; forward-thinking statements; considerably detailed; significant legal, financial, fiduciary, and regulatory impact implication

Once classified, the plan's matrix maps the source of the information request (i.e., line employee, supplier, Wall Street analyst, customer, etc.) and the anticipated point of contact for that source. Finally, by overlaying the level designations onto the contacts and ultimate sources of answers, considerable clarity is created. Once refined and rolled out, this process ensures that anyone in the organization is clear about who is authorized to answer what questions.

Anticipating specific questions and scripting the answers is frequently underrated in organizations in distress. While most probably have FAQ processes, the uniqueness of the circumstances prompts questions unique to these circumstances. Creating a comprehensive list of questions that would be reasonably expected from each audience identified and then scripting the answers ensures consistency and efficiency.

CONTROL THE MESSAGE OR IT WILL CONTROL YOU

Consistency enhances credibility. Particularly during challenging stages of growth, credibility is essential. Consequently, the content of responses requires careful deliberation. This dilemma is a primary culprit when understanding why many organizations fail to develop and execute comprehensive communication strategies. A consistent message that is clear, responsibly transparent, and respectful reduces the potential for noisy notes to be introduced to the score.

Remember, there will be many questions. If those questions are not answered satisfactorily, the audience will fill in the gaps. A sensible communication strategy will create music with the information and eliminate the noise. Silence is not golden. They will not "just trust" their leaders to protect their lives. Controlling the message is always better than allowing the message to control you.

Conclusion

The Mic Drop

Harmony. Hum. Purr. Whatever the metaphor, a key obligation of leaders is to take responsible measures to ensure the organization is performing optimally and efficiently. Whether the organization operates in the private sector or the public sector, is for profit or nonprofit, the universal imperative to create music, not noise, is paramount. The most astute leaders possess a unique talent for creating harmony and adeptly recognizing the subtle sources that add noise to the music.

No organization is immune to adversity. Market conditions are dynamic. Demand and competition intensify pressure. Innovation accelerates nimbleness. Rapidly evolving environments demand constant and equally rapid adaptability. Effective organizations adapt effectively, often on the leading edge of change rather than in response. Tone-deaf leaders allow their organizations to accept stagnancy, which makes customers, stakeholders, employees, and partners cringe. Whether it is the cause or the symptom, stagnancy produces noise. Most leaders are competent and make choices they are confident are in the best interest of the organization. However, tone-deaf leaders miss the subtle cues that systematically disrupt harmony, often resulting in existential challenges. The key to recognizing these subtle cues is knowing where to look and listen without misinterpreting what we see and hear.

The subtle cues that contribute to noisy performance are rarely obvious in financial reports, business school lectures, management

CONCLUSION

books, and seminars. Although they constantly exist, these cues are difficult to recognize or understand for a variety of reasons that typically occur in bunches. These are time-induced contributors—attitudes, approaches, behaviors, and perspectives—that become part of the organizational ethos. Success and failure are both affected by diverse controllable and uncontrollable conditions. How leaders respond to these conditions determines the organization's survivability. Beyond the more obvious performance indicators, key attitudes, practices, and behaviors often go unnoticed but play a significant role in the creation of music or noise. The list is extensive but contains some commonalities:

- Pervasive overconfidence that leads to arrogance at personal and organizational levels blinds leaders to potentially destructive weaknesses and exposes organizations to adversity. No one is immune to adversity. Get over yourself. Force realism enterprise-wide.
- Adversity generates activity. Considerable energy can be invested in activities addressing superficial rather than actual problems. Take the time to assess and solve the right problem.
- Comfort and complacency promote tone-deafness and inhibit creative perspective. When adversity strikes, this myopia prompts leaders to apply familiar solutions—most of which contribute to the adversity. Think counterintuitively. Use the unique perspectives from all of your tools to truly find the most effective solutions.
- Cultural mediocrity is like a cherished easy chair. It is easy to fall into and hard to get out of. Pervasive mediocrity is obscured by often misleading and manipulated results, convincing leaders that theirs is a convocation of eagles rather than a rafter of turkeys. Listen for gobbles. Look for the unemployed on the payroll.
- Organizations often find even the simplest activities to have become overly and unnecessarily complicated over the years. The result is an abundance of hardworking staff

exhausting themselves to complete tasks that could and should be done more smartly. Honor those who work hard. Value those who work smart. Treasure those who work hard *and* smart.
- Constant change and innovative drive are only successful when they improve the lives of the customers first. The momentum of myopic innovation and simple boredom can unknowingly distract organizations, creating noise when the customer is listening to music. Make sure all actions consider the real customer before considering organizational benefits. More importantly, make sure the choices reflect those you exist to serve. The fastest way to lose constituents is to lose touch with them.
- Internal practices easily distract focus at all levels. Distraction results in unproductive and costly noise from every section. One of the most common characteristics of successful organizations is their adherence to their DNA—a discipline that never loses sight of the core purpose—what they do and how they do it. Conversely, organizations that lose their way tend to, first, lose sight of what they really do. Make sure all activities connect directly to the core focus of the organization.
- Indecision is both a significant cause and symptom of adversity. Adversity often causes paralysis. Paralysis inhibits effective decision-making and action. Lead. Follow. Or get out of the way! Highways are lined with flat squirrels who could not make up their minds.
- Market conditions demand constant progress. Unfocused activities can divert focus on core constituent requirements, creating attention-consuming initiatives that are more superficial than substantive. Focus on steak before sizzle.
- Functions and activities easily grow over the lifespan of an organization. This gradual growth can easily consume valuable resources that rarely demonstrate a direct contribution to profitability. When adversity strikes, difficult decisions

CONCLUSION

are made to ensure that limited resources are deployed to the right places. Prioritization is excruciatingly difficult without a simple, objective perspective. Every investment should either make you money or save you money.

- Road maps show us how to get to our destination. Many organizations fail to recognize the importance of processes or overcomplicate processes to the point of rendering them ineffective. Often, existing practices seem so natural their processes are ignored. Shortcuts are abundant. Noise is created from even the simplest functions and procedures. Process makes perfect. Perfect the processes.
- The jungle is crowded with predators hunting a constantly narrowing source of prey. Passive offensive and defensive business development activities are the quickest way to fall behind the competition. Every organization has a competitor. Period. You eat what you kill. Hunt wisely. Defend diligently. Consume efficiently.
- Conflict, confusion, chaos, and curiosity lead to questions requiring truthful and consistent answers. When these answers are unavailable, people fill in the blanks themselves. This *never* goes well. While determining what to say and who should say it can be sensitive, a strategic communication strategy is critically important to ensure consistency and credibility. Control the message, or it will control you.

Despite good intentions, many of the tone-deaf failed to recognize these cues, and their attempts to correct negative trends fell short. Caused by a variety of factors, the absence of holistic and dimensional evaluation consistently results in noise. Effective leadership demands dimensional assessments and inspires decisive solutions to eliminate the cause as well as the symptom. The effective leader identifies the sour notes and disparate musicians and inspires a harmonious energy that ultimately produces music, not noise. And their audiences applaud.

About the Author

G. Robert "Bob" James, chairman of Solomon Group International, is a distinguished figure in the world of corporate development. With over three decades of experience, he specializes in turnaround management, organizational development, and growth strategies, serving a diverse clientele, including Fortune 100 companies and heads of foreign states. Additionally, he has served on the boards of several organizations in both the public and private sectors. A recognized authority on leadership during challenging times, Bob's expertise has been instrumental in guiding various entities through adversity.

In addition to his role at Solomon, Bob has held senior executive positions in public companies such as the Estée Lauder Companies, the Great Atlantic and Pacific Tea Company (A&P), and Royal Ahold. His contributions span portfolio strategy, global insights, international business development, and corporate expansion, particularly in APAC, EMEA, and South America.

Beyond his corporate achievements, Bob's commitment to community and international causes shines through. He has dedicated his life to improving the well-being of children, collaborating with organizations like the Muscular Dystrophy Association, St. Jude's Hospital, and the Food Bank of New York, among others. His philanthropic efforts extend to global initiatives to brighten the future for generations to come.

Bob's journey is marked by academic accomplishments at the bachelor and graduate levels, as well as accolades for achievement from organizations around the world, making him a prominent figure in the world of corporate development and humanitarian endeavors.

Printed in the USA
CPSIA information can be obtained
at www.ICGtesting.com
CBHW031530171024
15901CB00050B/635